The Angel Valley Labyrinth

FIRST EDITION

MIKE DAVIS

DEDICATION

This material was researched extensively in many ways as part of "Legends of the Verde Valley" and is dedicated to those who often are not able to make the pilgrimage to the *Holy Land* in person. This work is the result of a dream/vision where there are doorways between heaven and earth in the Red Rock mountains of Arizona. To have found some very conclusive evidence there is something supernatural going on in the region from personal accounts it has become very apparent these doorways exist leading to a greater understanding of the nature of the world we live in and ourselves.

CONTENTS

ACKNOWLEDGMENTS

Would like to personally thank all those who helped with putting the pieces of the puzzle together and making the publication possible especially my wonderful wife, family, and others working behind the scenes making the impossible possible. *"There's more to the Labyrinth phenomena than most realize. Herein lies a few clues about the nature of few of those magical places in particular."*

Additionally, by no means am I a writing guru or did I have the time at this point to proofread the material over 100 plus time looking for every mistake. There will be a grammatical error here and there. Don't let it get to you for the message is far greater than anything else. And this is just the start...

1 THE LABYRINTH, MANDALA, AND MAZE

Labyrinths and labyrinthine symbols have been found in diverse regions all throughout the world over the ages, some dating clear back to the *Neolithic Age.* The word itself appears to of come from the Greek *labyrinthos* describing any maze-like structure with a single path through it leading to a center.

Labyrinths and mazes have a lot in common and are by all means closely related. In colloquial English, the labyrinth is generally synonymous with maze. In the broader sense, a maze is also a labyrinth, but strictly spoken a labyrinth is not a maze since one cannot get lost in it. The difference between mazes and labyrinths is that mazes have multiple paths which branch off and will not necessarily lead to the center whereby labyrinths have a single continuous path that leads to the center, and as long as you keep going forward, you will get there eventually.

Traditionally, labyrinths feature a unicursal path with no dead-ends or false openings while mazes consist of multiple blind alleys leading a person where the creator intended. Mazes are designs in which the participant is confronted with many choices or paths to get to the goal. As such it is basically a problem-solving puzzle. Garden mazes are usually created with tall hedges a person cannot see over or see-through, making it difficult to navigate from the entrance to the exit.

Image above: Girolamo Frigimelica's maze at Villa Pisani near Venice, Italy. *(Public domain.)*

Therefore, it should be clear a maze is a complex branching (multicursal) puzzle that includes choices of path, direction, often having multiple entrances/exits, and dead ends. Mazes tend to trap and trick; labyrinths, on the other hand, are a tool for walking meditation winding a person into a center without any obstacles, and then allow them to return. Mazes are a relatively recent invention, first appearing around 600 years ago in the gardens of royal places and wealthy landowners in late medieval Europe.

Walking the labyrinth balances the left and right sides of the brain, and induces a centered and calm state of being. Labyrinths are about the journey, at least as much as the destination. They can be calming, as they slow you down while you wind your way through the path. There is only one way in and one way out, so you don't need to think about where you're going. The whole path of the labyrinth takes place within a circle; and circles are symbols of wholeness, and center, for they have no beginning or end. "The Celts described the labyrinth as the Never-Ending Circle."

In the Middle Ages, walking a cathedral labyrinth was a substitute for going on a pilgrimage to Jerusalem, the Holy Land leading to one's destiny. During those times not everyone could make the long and arduous journey, so walking a labyrinth in a church thus became a devotional activity. As a person travels through the labyrinth, they normally would become increasingly lost in reference to the world outside and, possibly, would unexpectedly discover one's true path in life.

"Caution—not all circuitous paths are labyrinths."

Mazes and labyrinths have been prominent components of European gardens and estates for centuries now gaining popularity in the U.S. Mazes have no particular spiritual significance it seems remarkably dropping off in England and other places throughout the 18th century. Today there are thousands of labyrinths in places all over the U.S. like houses of worship, medical centers, and public parks. More than 100 hospitals, hospices, and health care facilities in the U.S. reportedly have walkable labyrinths.

Mandalas can be found in all the ancient cultures even in Christianity as expressed at the Chapel of St. Zeno. *(Public domain.)*

Mandalas were created in the service of one of the world's great religions, Buddhism. Within art history, they are found in ancient Tibetan writing and sketches (8th-9th centuries) and on cloth paintings and murals of religious sanctuaries (11th– 12th centuries). Religions like Hinduism, Buddhism, Jainism, and Shintoism all believed in the Mandala and its symbolism of holy purpose. In the Tantric texts of India, the labyrinth is often featured and found in the design of mandalas.

Mandala is a Sanskrit word that loosely translates to mean *"circle"* or *"center."* In the Hindu and Buddhist traditions, mandalas are an object of meditation to aid in one's spiritual development employed for focusing attention as a spiritual guidance tool for the purpose of establishing a sacred space. *"In the center of the mandala lies the palace, which has four gates oriented to the four quarters of the world."*

Mandala art has been popularized by American visionary artist *Alex Grey;* a Vajrayana practitioner who believes the practice of artistic creation facilitates enlightenment.

Image above: The *Sri Yantra*, or Shri Chakra, a form of a mystical diagram (yantra) used in the Shri Vidya school of Hinduism consisting of interlocking triangles surrounding a central point (These triangles represent the cosmos and the human body) and the Mandala of *Jnanadakini. (Public domain.)*

10

Mandala has over time become a word that is synonymous with sacred space. These intricately created visual guides take a person on a journey reminding the viewer of the sacred universe in all and in oneself. In pre-Buddhist philosophical texts, the mandala signifies a sacred enclosure created for the performance of a particular ritual or practice, or for the use of a great teacher or mystic.

"The mandala is an archetypal image whose occurrence is attested throughout the ages. It signifies the wholeness of the Self. This circular image represents the wholeness of the psychic ground or, to put it in mythic terms, the divinity incarnate in man." — Carl Jung

One of the training tools in Tibetan mysticism is the use of the mandala on a person's spiritual and psychological growth. A teacher creates a mandala containing the symbols and deities the trainee needs to evolve along the path. When complete, the trainee walks the mandala stopping at different stations meditating. To be able to complete the mandala means completion of work on the inner self.

Mandala work is very useful in therapy. In spiritual traditions throughout the world, mandalas focus and reflect the spiritual content of the psyche for both the creator and the viewer. It has been surmised image archetypes at times emerge spontaneously when people are in the healing process brought on either in artwork or in dreams.

Carl J. Jung, a Swiss psychiatrist introduced to the West the practice of creating mandalas for self-discovery, expression, and healing. Carl Jung used the word *"magic circle,"* to describe the circular drawings he and his patients created. In Jung's work with his clients, he would sometimes have them draw mandalas for therapy observing through creating mandalas patients were better able to experience chaotic psychological states.

Just how important is the mandala? Someone or something wanted the people in the sky to view one on earth. Over the years many have wondered what the exact purpose of the mysterious Nazca lines is meant to be which oddly can only be truly seen from above. What were the ancient's trying to say with these messages?

Perhaps the most enigmatic depictions of Nazca are what is known as the Mandala. According to some claims, scientists from the University of Dresden researched the Nazca lines, measuring the magnetic field and electric conductivity and discovering that electric conductivity was 8000 higher on the Nazca lines than next to them.

The Mandala is considered a ritual symbol in Indian religions representing the universe in a geometrical pattern that represents the cosmos symbolizing the notion that life is, in fact, a never-ending cycle. The Ancient Hindus are said to be among the first people on the planet to use a Mandala spiritually, but the most famous Mandala most of us know are in fact made by Buddhists.

"The Edge labyrinth in Hogsback, South Africa is one mile long."

The labyrinth/mandala is composed of a number of symbols striking profound chords in the subconscious. It is through these archetypal forms the labyrinth/mandala is found to be linked to man's inner world, to the Jungian collective unconscious. Under close analysis, Jung remarkably identified universal patterns and archetypes which can appear in dreams and visions or can be created spontaneously as drawing. This knowledge helped enabled him to identify emotional disorders and work towards wholeness in personality realizing there was a great deal of similarity in the images they created. Jung intimately associated the drawings with psychological and spiritual health. When a mandala image appeared in a patient's artwork or dreams, he found it usually indicated progress toward new self-knowledge. *Jung stated that the mandala is the archetype of wholeness, relating it to the Self.*

Inscribed on a column in the temple of Delphi were three of the Delphic maxims of the Seven Sages: ΓΝΩΘΙ ΣΕΑΥΤΟΝ (KNOW THYSELF), ΜΗΔΕΝ ΑΓΑΝ (NOTHING IN EXCESS), and ΕΓΓΥΑ, ΠΑΡΑ ΔΑΤΗ (SURETY BRINGS RUIN).

For many centuries philosophers and theologians have wrestled with the question of whether or not reality is a dream, or whether we are dreamers or the dreamed. In Hermetic tradition, we are both being the thoughts and dreams of infinite Mind. As microcosms of the macro, we are also dreamers. Socrates stated: "To know thyself is the beginning of wisdom." It appears the ancient writings were pointing toward the nature of everything, *"Know thyself, and thou shalt know the universe and God."*

2 ORIGINS OF THE LABYRINTH

It is said the exact origin of the labyrinth is to date unknown according to the academic history we have available. However, there are some intricate details found in some of the world's most notorious labyrinth legends which could of course perhaps point in the possible direction as to whom very well may have possibly built such elaborate structures and why.

Finding out who built the labyrinth and why it's important for it will surely help us understand how to better use them properly. Much of what we do know about these mysterious structures has been buried over time hidden. The earliest literary reference to the term labyrinth was found on a Mycenaean clay tablet at Knossos, dated 1400 BC. The text on the tablet was translated to be:

"One jar of honey to all the gods, one jar of honey to the Mistress of the Labyrinth."

Pictures of ancient labyrinths can be found all over the world inscribed on rock carvings, petroglyphs and elaborate inscriptions clearly showing the influence these magical symbols had in history. One of the most famous labyrinths of the ancient world was housed in an Egyptian pyramid complex built in the 12th Dynasty (1844-1797 B.C.) at Hawara by Amenemhet III.

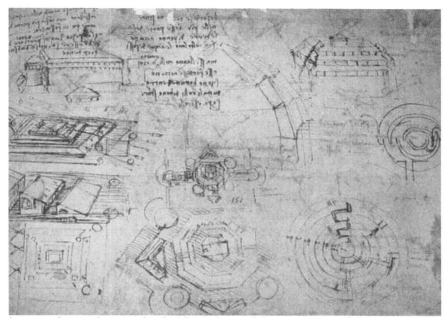

Image above: *Leonardo de Vinci drew elaborate mazes/labyrinths in his artwork. He also constructed drawings (over 200 with different angels and proportions with descriptions of each one) specifically relating to the Flower of Life. (Public domain.)*

Leonardo da Vinci was a true genius who graced this world with his presence credited for designing a one-of-a-kind automated humanoid in 1495 along with other interesting art works seemed on the objective to find the one true path for enlightenment.

The greatest well-known labyrinth is found in Greek mythology as an elaborate, confusing structure designed and built by the legendary artificer Daedalus for *King Minos* of Crete at Knossos. The mystical serpentine structure was said to of held a dreaded half man and half beast Minotaur that fed on seven virgin men and seven virgin girls from Athens often to keep it contained. These tributes would then be placed in the Labyrinth for the Minotaur to devour.

In various sources, the sacrificial victims were chosen by lot from only the most beautiful men and virginal girls. The Athenians consulted the Oracle of Delphi who instructed the city of Athens to give Minos whatever he demanded. According to this legend, Daedalus had so cunningly and skillfully made the Labyrinth that he could barely escape it after he built it. However, as a prison for the Minotaur, a labyrinth would have been extremely inexpedient.

It must be duly noted only a maze with its dead ends and the bewildering paths could have been suited to hold a supernatural creature. Labyrinths are not mazes. Maze's trap and trick; labyrinths are a walking spiritual meditation winding a person deep into a center without any obstacles and then allowed to return.

During Minos' reign, Daedalus, took up residence in Knossos, after he was exiled to Crete where he eventually became the official architect and sculptor for Minos building the Palace, the Labyrinth, and later even helped Ariadne and Thiseas kill the horrible flesh-eating Minotaur monster.

Then for whatever reason, at some point, Minos became disillusioned with Daedalus and jailed him together with his son, Icarus. However, the brilliant engineer with his mysterious abilities didn't stay long-imprisoned making a pair of wings for himself and Icarus who then somehow flew away. The strange wings were said to be made of feathers held together with special wax. The two successfully flew from Crete, but Icarus began getting careless while soaring in the sky flying too close to the sun where the wax holding together the feather on his wings melted causing him to fall to his death.

The story from beginning to the end indeed has some very interesting twists and turns. When taking a closer look at its dialog as being the earliest known reference to labyrinths/mazes we find the presence of the ancient gods. Back then the mixing of man and beast was something associated with the *Watcher Angels* for there are aspects within the tale that clearly signify the presence of arcane abilities which are like a fingerprint. *"These are the Watchers (Grigori), who turned aside from the Lord, 200 myriads, together with their prince Satanail." 2 Enoch 18:3*

The Book of Enoch leaves no doubt that it was the offspring of unnatural unions that brought about the need for God to wipe out mankind with a flood mostly due to the creation of those who were feasting on human flesh as a result of unlawful unions on earth. These beings were said to be soulless afterward from the unlawful union becoming disenchanted spirits.

These mythological hybrid zoomorphic deities are found in the folklore of a variety of cultures as legendary beings who are given an anthropomorphic aspect. The motif of the winged man is taken up in the Etruscan Vanth, Assyrian winged genie, Hellenistic Eros-Amor, and ultimately the Christian iconography of angels. It is clear the ferocious half-man/half-bull Minotaur appearing in *Dante's Inferno* and the modern comic character *"Hell Boy"* that an otherworldly presence was therein making not all labyrinths/mazes the same.

Whether or not the mythical tale is true is up to each person to discover for themselves. Finding out the first Labyrinths have mysterious roots which history claims are connected to the Gods who according to legend not only created some of them but also closely guard the important ones as well is perhaps a clue as to their importance in the past and today.

Mentioned by William Shakespeare in *"A Midsummer-Night's Dream,"* and employed as a dancing ground for rustic festivities, labyrinths were once widespread. Did you know there are approximately 6,000 labyrinths registered worldwide today?

What area of the world has the highest concentration of labyrinths? Bolshoi Zayatsky Island has 14 in less than 1/2 square mile. Nobody knows who built the place estimated to be over 2500 years old.

"There are things known, and things unknown, and between are the doors." Aldous Huxley

The Trolleborg Labyrinth

17

In Swedish folklore "The Blue Virgin" Island was seen as a supernatural place where evil spirits cursed by witchcraft dwelled, and it was best avoided by sailors. According to legend, it was thought that witches would regularly meet on the island to worship those associated with the devil and giants. The largest labyrinth in Sweden, made of stone, little is known about it. No one knows when it was built, or by whom. What is known is that setting up labyrinths in the archipelago was rather common in the past.

Although the function of the stone settings may be unclear, some have suggested is that they may have symbolized a border between this world and other worlds like the underworld and the labyrinth may have been used for specific rituals to help the souls of the dead travel to those other worlds.

No one knows why so many ancient labyrinths were built on this tiny northern island on Russia's Sea less than one square mile in total, but is covered in over a dozen of labyrinths dated as far back as 30,000 B.C. Archaeologists have been unable to pin down the exact purpose of the labyrinths, but the overall consensus to date appears to be that they were used for mystical reasons which some suggest include a portal to the underworld, a trap for evil spirits, or the altar for ceremony. For whatever the reason, it's clear from the types of ruins present that *Bolshoi Zayatsky Island* was once a place for magical operations, though we may never know exactly to what extent or of what kind.

It's clear from some structures found in the world there was not only advanced math used to create the mysterious megalithic stone places like the pyramids, labyrinths, etc., but are also visibly encoded with some truths which have truly stood the test of time. No flood, earth quakes, or other events have been able to erase these facts of stone off from the face of the earth to date. What remains, on the other hand, is a lot more questions than answers. Nevertheless, there very well may be some clues as to whom very well may have built a few labyrinths and why.

The Wheel of Giants Labyrinth

Visible only from the air because of its size one of the most mysterious structures in the Middle East is the prehistoric stone monument in the Golan Heights known as *Rujm el-Hiri*. Its Hebrew name is Gilgal Refaim, or "*Wheel of Giants*" and "*Wheel of Spirits*" or "*Wheel of Ghosts*" referring to an ancient race of giants mentioned in the Bible.

The location is notably just north (19 miles) of *Mount Hermon* (also called the *Mountain of Transfiguration* housing a *United Nations* radar outpost) where in the *Book of Enoch* some 200 *Watcher Angels* were said to of descended to earth from heaven teaching mankind forbidden technology. Close by is the *Alter of Pan*, *Gates of Hades*, and also the *Fortress of Nimrod* who attempted to a one world government and build a tower in order to slay the Creator. *Is it just a coincidence all these other supernatural places and beings are located in the region next to this mountain range? The mountain is also where Christ took the disciples before his epic battle with the devil preaching about his death and resurrection where he said upon this rock, I will build my church.*

Some have surmised the structure was used to communicate with the dead. By the very name Rephaim some say this is the center of the worship of the dead and the spirits of the dead. The structure clearly took some rather large beings, won't call them people, some time to construct.

In Genesis 14:5, the Refaim inhabit the place called Ashtherot-Karnaim and according to history were a powerful tribe being as tall as the Anakim (giants). The strange pattern of stone circles was spotted by archaeologists studying an aerial survey of the Golan Heights after 1967 war.

In Chronicles 20, there is further mention of this race where the last of the Anakim is killed.

"And yet again there was war at Gath, where was a man of great stature, whose fingers and toes were four and twenty, six on each hand, and six on each foot: and he also was the son of the giant. But when he defied Israel, Jonathan the son of Shimea David's brother slew him. These were born unto the giant in Gath; and they fell by the hand of David, and by the hand of his servants."

The Mount of Olives is first mentioned in bible, "And David went up by the ascent of the Mount of Olives and wept as he went up." It's also mentioned as the place where Christ stood when he wept over Jerusalem. Perhaps its biggest attribute is its known as a sacred site whereby in the story of David it was a place of worship for YHVH. An apocalyptic prophecy in the Book of Zechariah states that

YHWH will stand on the Mount of Olives and the mountain will split in two, with one half shifting north and one half shifting south. Without question the location is very important where God promises to meet his people which it has been throughout history, still is today, and will be in the future according to ancient text.

Of course, the adversary also knows the importance of the mount of divine presence as well having constructed the "Mount of Corruption" overlooking the place not far away. In the last week of his life Christ spend his time at two distinct specific locations teaching in the temple and then to the Mount of Olives where he taught the disciples. Christ was crucified and buried at the place, descended into the abyss proclaiming to prisoners there according to Peter, then taken up into heaven there, and is said to be returning to the same location as well. The importance of the place is without question.

Not far away within walking distance Christ also went up to Mount Hermon the place where the Watchers had set themselves up. Christ climbed Mount Hermon with 3 disciples and was transformed into a being of light at the location letting the powers and 72 principalities know he was there whereby from then on, those powers would be subject to his name. The high mountain top is where according to ancient text the god "El" held court with his 72 sons, the gods of the nations, 72 cosmos creators, the 72 stars inside the rotunda capitol dome in Washington called "the Apotheosis of Washington." Isaiah 14: 12-14 remarkably states:

"For you have said in your heart: I will ascend into heaven, I will exalt my throne above the stars of God; I will also sit on the Mount of Congregation on the farthest side of the north; I will ascend above the heights of the clouds, I will be like the most high."

The 40,000 tons of basalt rock maze of ruins is said to be up to 5,000 years old and all proposed solutions are only more or less likely theories as to its purpose to date. However, the Bible makes a clear connection to the *Watcher Angels* being involved which is something which must be duly noted. The structure is perhaps the largest labyrinth/maze found to date with comparisons with Stonehenge in England, the pyramids in Egypt, the Nazca Lines in Peru, and even the huge statues on Easter Island would not be unfair. No doubt the location was an important site on a global scale and still is today.

Image above: A cow attempts to get around a huge 15-foot-high labyrinth of stone constructed next to Mount Hermon. *(Public domain.)*

There is no real academic notion of what they truly are or why they are here but scientists, archaeologists, and others agree that this enormous enigmatic stone structure is one of the oldest and largest in the region. But that's about all they can agree on. Dr. Uri Berger, an expert on megalithic structures with the Israel Antiquities Authority says no-one knows who built it – another parallel to Stonehenge, the purpose of which has remained a mystery for millennia.

"We have bits of information, but not the whole picture. Scientists come and are amazed by the site and think up their own theories."

Under close observation the question that keeps cropping up is a simple one: *how is it possible that such a fascinating place exists yet remains inaccessible and almost unknown? Is this perhaps the most ancient labyrinth to date built by the Watcher Angels and their offspring? Could this mysterious place be some kind of an ancient transporter pad for consciousness like in Star Trek to the adobe of the gods?*

Another interesting coincidence connected to this site is the fact it is also remarkably just under 1/4 mile from where *Elijah* was said to be taken up into heaven. *Why would there be a legend of God taking someone up into heaven with this location?* There sure is a whole lot of supernatural activity connected to this site. Is this where the gates of heaven were at one time open and are now mysteriously closed? *"Have the gates to heaven been sealed?"*

Let there be no question someone went through a great amount of time to construct the mysterious place for an unknown reason. *It seems the secrets of these place are not known to the public.* The structure would seem to be an ancient place where some kind of strange ceremonies were taken place.

It must be duly noted it was the *Watcher Angels* who were the ones said to have given the secrets of heaven away to the inhabitants of earth by rebelling from their first adobe or estate (heaven). According to legend, these beings not only knew of heaven by living there but they also knew how to travel back and forth between earth and the adobe of the gods.

"I believe legends and myths are largely made of truth." - J.R.R. Tolkien (There's more truth is his books than most realize.)

The etymology of labyrinth has two interlinked variations: 1) derived from labrys, a pre-Hellenic word said to mean 'double headed axe', 2) derived from the Latin labia meaning 'lips' or 'folds'. The double-headed axe was sacred to Zeus, the Grecian Thor, whose hammer was a variant of the labrys when spinning formed the shape of the swastika or Vortex.

There are of course other locations which stand out as being what some call vagina-shaped ritual caves. Gobekli Tepe in Turkey is estimated at 11,000 years old, assessed to be perhaps the oldest temple on Earth. There seem to be carving on the stones that are star constellations leading the initiate along a self-transformative journey on these power points that our ancestors built to be used as part of their ceremonial and spiritually transformative work used clearly as a portal to the universe.

There are of course portals to the Universe which have been intricately constructed and placed in astronomical alignment may have once opened portals to the stars permitting entry for entities from other worlds and dimensions. It appears ancient sages knew very well the laws of this universe and how those laws manifest in this planet.

These places according to some were built for practices that allowed them to access otherworldly dimensions which are beyond time placing one in contact with the *Ancestors*. The mysterious site for some strange reason had been deliberately covered over with soil and abandoned perhaps due to being too powerful. There are some mysteries/legends that are perhaps not meant to be solved, because the mystery in itself is a key that would open some of the blocks in the subconscious mind.

3 TYPES OF LABYRITHS

Since the dawn of civilization, the labyrinth symbol has been an integral part of many myths, religions, and rituals. Examining some of these narratives reveals how the labyrinth may have affected diverse spiritual orientations in order to create an emerging system whereby blending Christian and New Age beliefs with Jungian theory.

Existing for at least 3500 years, the archetypal labyrinth design is found in both circular and square forms. Found in historical contexts throughout Europe, North Africa, and other places the design has even been found to occur in the American Southwest. Practically all labyrinths prior to the first few centuries BCE are of this type displaying archetypal symbolism. Although the subsequent association with the legendary Labyrinth at Knossos is well documented, the design certainly predates the legend.

Image above: Circular and square varieties of the classical labyrinth design. *(Public domain.)*

Basically, there are two primary labyrinth designs: the 7-circuit Classical labyrinth and the 11-circuit Chartres labyrinth type. (Circuits refer to how many times the path spirals before reaching the center.) The classical labyrinth is considered pre-Christian in design and the *Chartres Labyrinth* is the design installed in many cathedrals during the Middle Ages in Europe. The labyrinth in Chartres Cathedral located in France is one of the few remaining intact cathedral labyrinths still in use today.

The 11-circuit Chartres Labyrinth was constructed sometime around 1201 AD when monks used it for contemplative moments sitting on the stone floor in France. Then shortly afterward medieval Christians often were said to visit Chartres (and other cathedrals) walking the labyrinth as an alternative to taking a hazardous pilgrimage to the *Holy Land* in Jerusalem to walk in the *"footsteps of Christ."* Going to an esteemed labyrinth became popular with those who could not go on long journeys like the disabled and elderly.

There have been many theories and elaborate mythology surrounding the original construction of the labyrinth. No one knows for sure exactly when the labyrinth was made, as no documents have yet been found, and little is known about who built it and why, but there are lots of signs. However, in 2001 some claim the center of the labyrinth was the site of a memorial or tomb for the cathedral labyrinth masons, but no evidence was found to back up such claims. Yet according to some the labyrinth of Chartres Cathedral, was built by the "Knights Templars" having at its center is the six-petaled "Plantagenet" or "Wild Rose." The Rose symbolism of the core of the labyrinth of Chartres appears to be an echo from the Garden of Solomon.

"At Chartres rose in the center can be seen bathed in the light of the sun beaming through a strategically placed pane of red stained glass, making the Grail symbolism apparent."

The Cathedral itself is a marvel of Gothic architecture and Romanesque styles designated a World Heritage Site by UNESCO, which calls it a masterpiece and "the high point of French Gothic art." Said to an important destination for many travelers since at least the 12th century, it notably remains so to the present, many of whom come to venerate its famous relic, the *Sancta Camisa*, said to be the tunic worn by the Virgin Mary at Christ's birth. *The concept of the labyrinth's power is often miraculous.*

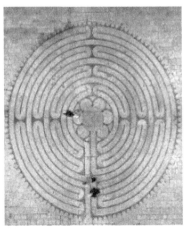

Image above: Coin from Knossos, Crete, c. 70 BCE and people walking the Chartres Labyrinth, France. *(Public domain.)*

The significance of some labyrinths throughout history is truly undeniable thriving on throughout the ages into modern times. Indeed, there seems to be something about these mysterious places besides being an elaborate structure that draws people from all walks of life into a center.

The conceptual depictions represent a journey with visible or invisible elements at times of entrapment or enlightenment, and sometimes both. The use of these places can be very diverse in purpose and meaning as in the entrapment of spirits, an enemy, a friend or even a lover. These journeys are said to be the enlightenment of knowledge, of the soul, and of the body. *For thousands of years, the labyrinthine figure has meant many different things to many different people.*

Roman Labyrinths

Much could be said about this Greek myth with its implications and elements. Labyrinths and minotaur's were not the usual choices for mosaic artists during the Roman period but for some mysterious reasons, at some point, it appeared. It is clear the Romans not only believed in the mysterious power labyrinths but developed some of their own some of which were square and occasionally polygonal, these labyrinths are found as mosaics on the floors of Roman buildings.

Image above: Roman Labyrinth, Vienna Art Museum. *(Public domain.)*

The Roman labyrinth varies somewhat from being square with an internal goal, 42 lanes in the area or in cross-section, 8 lanes center area, and 17 lanes or 17 turns in each quadrant with a central figure (of Theseus killing the Minotauros).

"Labyrinths were symbolic of the involvement and illusions of the lower world through which wanders the soul of man in its search for truth. In the labyrinth dwells the lower animal man with the head of a bull (the Minotaur or Serapis), who seeks to destroy the soul entangled in the maze of worldly ignorance. In this relation, Serapis (the Minotaur) becomes the Tryer or Adversary who tests the souls of those seeking union with the Immortals." ~ Manly P. Hall

Egyptian Labyrinths

The few clues that we have indicate that the Labyrinth originally was used for many different purposes to the Egyptians where they would make daily offerings to Amenemhet's spirit—for all eternity—in the hope of guaranteeing his prosperity in the afterlife. The Egyptian Labyrinth was more than 1,300 years old at the time when the ancient Greek historian Herodotus visited one giving quite the description.

"I visited this building and found it to surpass description; for if all the great works of the Greeks could be put together in one, they would not equal this Labyrinth. The Pyramids likewise surpass description, but the Labyrinth surpasses the Pyramids." —Herodotus, 5th century BC

Recorded in history Herodotus also related that the lower levels of the Labyrinth contained the "*sepulchers of the kings who built the Labyrinth and those of the sacred crocodiles.*" An interesting note when Egyptians became known to have buried sacred bulls in winding underground passages beneath other temples.

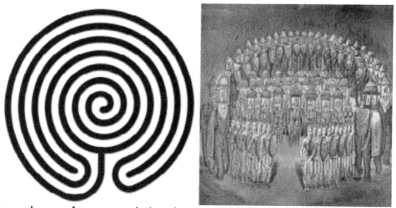

Image above: An unusual development of the classical labyrinth often drawn with a spiral at the center found primarily in India. It is referred to in Indian tradition as Chakra-vyuha, a name derived from a magical troop formation employed by the magician Drona at the battle of Kurukshetra recounted in the Mahabharata epic. *(Public domain.)*

Examples of labyrinths and the variations thereof can at times be somewhat thought-provoking. Taking the use of the symbol further was mysterious the *Padmavyūha*, a multitiered defensive formation that looks like a blooming lotus or disc (chakra) when viewed from above. The special military formation was used to surround enemies as depicted in the Hindu tradition.

Located on the front of the *Phoenix Cement Plant* in Clarkdale, Arizona is "*The Man in the Maze.*" *(Public domain.)*

I'itoi or I'ithi referred to as the "Man in the Maze," a reference to a design appearing on O'odham basketry and petroglyphs in Arizona. This labyrinth is believed by the Akimel O'odham and Tohono O'odham to be the maze of life, where a person travels through and encounters the different moments that impact them. In the middle of the maze, a person finds their dreams and goals. Tohono O'odham means "desert people" who have lived in the Sonoran Desert of southern Arizona and northern Mexico for centuries.

The origins of labyrinth symbols in the American Southwest are shrouded in mystery still with no archeological evidence to trace these intercontinental connections to where they originated. These symbols form important themes in the traditional stories of the Hopi and early pre-Pueblo peoples. There has been a nice display of an elaborate ancient Native American labyrinth petroglyph carved in stone in Case Grande, Arizona. The date of its formation or who might have created it and why remain unclear, however, the fact the symbol has been found throughout Arizona in many forms has been a sign for many of its importance.

Labyrinth or Maze inside Casa Grande, circa 1949. NPS photo (CG-128)

No question circles in stone have been found all over the world going back an estimated 15,000 years or more in regions like South Africa which can only be seen from the air. For unknown reasons, someone placed 1,000's of stone circles in places like Lebanon, Syria, Saudi Arabia and more. Nobody knows who made them or why including the Bedouins. Some have speculated a few of these mysterious places are Neolithic stone computers acting as transporter pads. The fact some stone structures have a recorded and measurable 10 Hertz wave pattern which just happens to be mysteriously the same of human brain patterns associated with relaxation, altered states of consciousness, and meditation is worthy of notice. *"Why are some of these mysterious stone places constructed to resonate with alpha brain patterns is the big question?"*

In pondering the ancient petroglyphs located at Cocoraque Butte, Arizona it is difficult to find people today who can interpret what they mean. On his visit to Cocoraque Butte, cultural expert *Joe Joaquin* explained that before the O'odham had a written language, petroglyphs were used as a means to transmit tribal traditions "We may not fully understand what the glyphs mean but they deserve respect as symbols of past traditions. You think of traditions when you see these sites." Joaquin noted that some petroglyphs seem to have been made when men marked what they saw on pilgrimages or spiritual quests.

Every time I look at a labyrinth site many try and think what ancient people were thinking when they drew these intricate pictures—what does it mean? *What were they thinking? What were the ancients trying to convey and why?"*

4 PRACTICAL USES OF LABTRINTHS

Since the early 1990s, interest in the use of labyrinths has spread over the years creating *labyrinth communities* who are a diverse group coming from different religious traditions, bringing different awareness, perspectives, skills, and experiences. The growing community has created a *World-Wide Labyrinth Locator* allowing people to search by country, city, state, and zip code. The listings include descriptions, directions, open hours, photos, and more.

Throughout the world, in the last decade, many labyrinths have been constructed in churches, hospitals, parks, prisons, and other areas. They have even been showing up in the backyards of homes for more personal use. These sacred places are often used by varying people for contemplation; tools for personal, psychological, and spiritual transformation, also thought to enhance right-brain activity. Universal commonality, which forms the basis of the community, is their belief in a higher power, and that the labyrinth ultimately creates a liminal or sacred space in which one can interact with that higher power.

As with most all symbols, something about the labyrinth points beyond itself leaving people to ponder in wonder, *"What does it mean?"* As with all symbols, each person must be willing to determine what it means for themselves. Labyrinths can be located indoors or out, permanent or temporary. Installations can feature different patterns to walk and can be simply a path mowed into the grass, painted on a portable canvas, or created with anything virtually anywhere.

Combining the imagery of the circle and the spiral into a meandering but purposeful path, the Labyrinth for most represents a journey to our own center and back again out into the world. (It has also been used as an act of repentance for sins. The penitent might crawl or walk the path on their knees.)

Entering the serpentine path of a labyrinth, a person walks slowly while quieting the mind and focusing on a spiritual question or prayer. The entrance to the labyrinth is called the mouth. The center of the labyrinth is called the goal, and when a person reaches it, they reverse steps, unwinding from the center out. Each step, each breath, every wind, ultimately leads to the center taking a person inward away from the outside into the sacred circle, the beginning and source.

Labyrinths have long been used as meditation and prayer tools when people wanted to get in touch with the divine or spirit world. Churches, retreat centers, and even Christian camps are using these prayer tools.

"It seems God has blessed the use of the labyrinth; many are being drawn closer experiencing healing and gaining spiritual clarity as they pray on its path."

Rumored to have originated from the gods some of these symbolic gateways seem to have manifested as an archetypal symbol showing us perhaps a labyrinth has power. Unlike many other archetypes, which remain abstract, people can physically get into and walk around in a labyrinth directly experiencing the energy within such a sacred space and place, taking one out of the ego, into the *"Deeper Self."*

Image above: *Tip o' The Hat Y'all...* Like the young lady said to the Man in Black, William in the HBO show *Westworld*. "You still don't understand the real game we are playing here. If you're looking forward, you are looking in the wrong direction." In the center of the maze, I find myself... A legend described as an "old native myth," in which the image of the maze is explained, "the sum of a man's life. The choices he makes, the dreams he hangs onto." *(Public domain.)*

There's a specific reason why the labyrinth of *Westworld* is found on the inside of the human skull. The show is very revealing about the nature of *Hollywood's* mind who has access to a variety of sources like psychologists along with *Artificial Intelligence*. Mazes are often used in psychology experiments to study the spatial navigation and learning typically using rats. "At times we are like rats in a maze."

In more recent years, much like in the ancient past, labyrinths/mazes have been expanded to much larger proportions in the film industry. The concept of mazes and labyrinths in media portray the allegory social experimentation in the realm of the consciousness/psyche to lab rats.

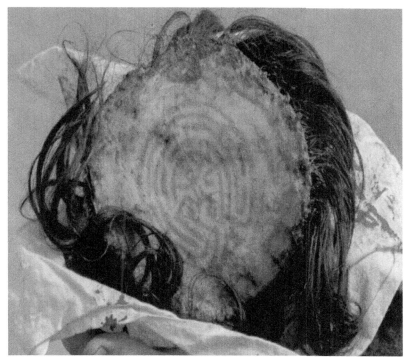

Image above: *Westworld* showed the labyrinth on the inside of the human scalp.

Typically used for therapeutic and healing, unlike the labyrinth, the Maze is used for the opposite, for confusion and disorientation. The Labyrinth is an ancient tool of illuminates, but the maze is an ancient tool of the Illuminati to deceive representing the rabbit hole or wormhole designed to confuse, subvert, and trap. One can find their way or get lost in their mind. When walked the tracing patterns of the labyrinth build neural networks and syncs the cognition in the hemispheres and lobes of the brain. When it is experienced outward within the macrocosm there is also a blueprint made inward within the micro. Yet the mystery goes even deeper straight into the human body.

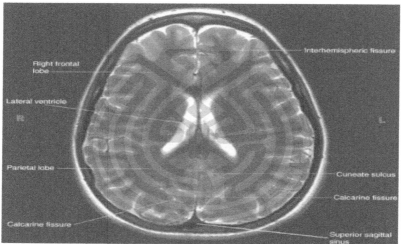

Image above: The Lateral Ventricle Labyrinth Man in the Maze" within the human brain.

The labyrinth to some seems like it's an exact layout of the human brain depicting the inside *lateral ventricles* which happens to be the location of the pineal body with neural pathways of the optic nerves around to the occipital lobe. *In a strange way there is indeed a man in the maze, a winged person.*

The universal purpose of the labyrinth is to find your way to the center and to find your way back out representing the process of involution and evolution whereby visiting the true self found at the very center. Walking the labyrinth is an external/internal simulacrum of the conscious mind.

One of the biggest keys to fully experiencing the effects of the labyrinth is to walk the path with bare feet making contact with the ground. This crucial step is often overlooked by most which is why it's often so important to have a person who has actually walked the walk to guide others safely on the path.

Labyrinth Facilitators

Over the last few decades, a body of knowledge about labyrinths, their history, and how to use them effectively has developed throughout the world. To date there is no set ritual for walking a labyrinth, each person must undertake the journey alone, but there are plenty of books and lectures to assist someone in performing a labyrinth walk. As with most things, it's always good to have a guide to assist along the way.

Labyrinth facilitators over the years have felt a calling to share this powerful tool with others. Their motivation is based on their own experiences and to provide a way for people to connect with the supernatural with which they believe they can interact. For some, the Labyrinth Walk is a purposeful guided prayer to get in touch with the source, while to others the place is a whole lot more.

For some, the labyrinth offers a way to connect with the spiritual realm not requiring the person to subscribe or even be aware of any particular belief system or religious faith. Establishing a connection to the supernatural within the labyrinth occurs as a result of taking the right steps beforehand then entering the mouth walking in a circuitous pattern integrating the left and right sides of the brain ultimately providing a whole-brain experience.

The practice of labyrinth walking is said to integrate the body with the mind and the mind with the spirit upon what some consider to be a divine imprint remarkably found in all religious traditions in various forms around the world. It's interesting to note how so many of the world's religions have utilized the use of labyrinths over time, which should be a clear indication of the potential benefits thereof.

The physical movement of the "walking prayer" can at times be soothing for a thirsting/troubled soul who desires to listen for the Holy Spirit. The journey is a walk which can be a *"Conversation with God,"* a rhythm of moving on a journey to lose distractions or resistances as a person journeys deeper into the center finding an invitation along the path to discovering the peace/presence inside.

Once the goal is met the return journey out becomes about what is God calling a person to do in the world and who the person is being called to become.

Image above: The supernatural roots of the labyrinth clearly show it to be connected to the gods. *(Public domain.)*

At the highest level, the labyrinth symbol works on several different but interconnected levels:

The Folds of Time,
The Spiral Cosmos,
The Folds of Human Self Deceit,
The Journey of Life,
The Brain and Spinal Column,
The Womb,
The Tomb or Creachaire,
The Vortex or Sumaire.

The labyrinth walking practice according to most facilitators integrates the body with the mind and the mind with the spirit of archetypal collective symbols transcending all cultures since they are grounded in the collective subconsciousness itself often linked to *Mandalas* - Sanskrit for *"circle that contains the essence."*

Finding out the Labyrinth has remarkably been a universal theme in all sagas leading a person to wonder why there is not more known regarding the subject. Within its twists and turns is the place of ritual, where all who enter walk on the same path. In these rituals, everything is symbolic for the Labyrinth closes up like an oyster closing upon itself when it hears too much noise pollution. Once the door is shut all sense of time gets emancipated vanishing away as the person walks around the spirals of the shell going deeper and deeper until one gets lost within the labyrinths echo in the ear leading further yet into the mind. The symbolic construct is, in fact, not paradoxical or a metaphor of existence, but is a path leading to our roots, to our own self, the very *"Garden of Eden"* within.

"People from all over the world travel to labyrinths not just to view the place in person, but to activate said place in mind/spirit within."

Many people have been looking for that one path, a path to guide personal existence to its ultimate, true goal of self-knowledge and expression. In the maze of life, many people have reached a dead-end with regards to everything material life has to offer where many are now looking for something completely different. Labyrinths symbolize the journey of life from birth to spiritual awakening. Lao Tzu spoke of "Tao", the Buddha spoke of the "eightfold way", the Bible speaks of the single one "narrow path."

"You're walking the labyrinth of life. Yes, you're meant to move forward, but almost never in a straight line. Yes, there's an element of achievement, of beginning and ending, but those are minor compared to the element of being here now. In the moments you stop trying to conquer the labyrinth of life and simply inhabit it, you'll realize it was designed to hold you safe as you explore what feels dangerous. You'll see that you're exactly where you're meant to be, meandering along a crooked path that is meant to lead you not onward, but inward." — Martha Beck

5 THE FLOWER OF LIFE (SACRED GEOMERTY)

Not all labyrinths are the same. A few have roots to the gods. Some labyrinths are said to contain non-verbal geometric and numerological prompts creating a field, in nature is multi-dimensional holographic, able to reveal the presence of a cosmic order within as they interface the world of material form and the subtler realms of higher consciousness. It is associated with the belief that a god is the "geometer" of the world. Sacred geometric patterns exist all around us throughout nature creating the fundamental structure and templates of all life in the universe.

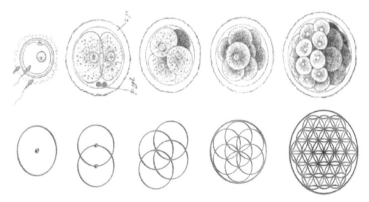

Image above: The beginning how life begins for humans with the first fertilized ovocyte. This symbol shows that all life and consciousness arise from one source (this being the first circle). The single cell then splits until we have the first seven circles (seed of life). *(Public domain.)*

The geometrical archetypes reveal an inseparable relationship between everything and everyone, which ultimately makes up the whole universe at large miraculously embodying oneness down to the single cell. Many religious teachings have described the Sacred Geometry theme as the blueprint (spirit) of creation and the origin of all forms. Spiraling within even further is the molecules of our DNA, the air we breathe, and all life forms that appear to have these geometric codes found throughout the known universe.

In ancient times, the experience of Sacred Geometry was essential to the education of the soul. These geometric codes are symbolic of our own inner realm, being significant to higher consciousness and states of being leading ultimately to self-awareness amplifying our connection to spirit creating harmony within as well as without.

The symbols are like codes assisting a person on their journey through life consciously bringing about deep soul connection in order to awaken to their true divine essence opening up pathways and doorways some mystics and ancient texts claim are to "infinite realms."

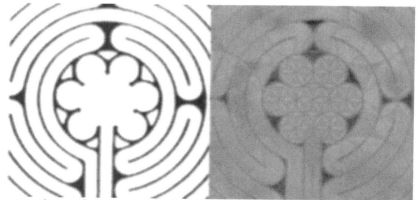

Image above: *Does the Chartres labyrinth in France contain the Flower of Life? (Public domain.)*

Indeed, there are and have been many different types, styles, and variations of the labyrinth throughout the ages but of all one, in particular, has stood out from all others for centuries. The motives behind one of the most enigmatic labyrinth depictions in the world is still a mystery to most common folk, but for some reason, it was built to be higher and bigger than other cathedrals of the era at 42 feet in diameter, the circular *Chartres Labyrinth* is the largest of its kind to have been constructed in the Middle Ages.

Image above: *The Rose Labyrinth has depths. (Public domain.)*

In alchemical drawings, the rose is a symbol of sacred space like a meditation chamber or altar. This sacred place is the mystical bridal chamber, the place of the mystic marriage, the mystic center of a person, his/her heart of hearts – one's true nature. It also represents the process of purification to reveal one's essence or the inner "pearl beyond price." Carl Jung put it: "The rose red color is related to the aqua permanens and the soul, which are extracted from the prima materia."

In Hebrew Qabalism, the center of the rose is the sun and the petals the infinite, but harmonious, diversities of Nature. The rose emanates and grows from the *Tree of Life*. According to the Kabbalistic book Zohar (Zohar means "light", "splendor") Rose is also considered a symbol of the people of Israel.

The Chartres Cathedral represents a very special window in time evident by its style and symbolism when great learning was still associated alongside religious intent representing the highest theological and philosophical aspirations of the era. The Chartres labyrinth was known as the "*Chemin de Jerusalem.*"

Of all the known labyrinths existing today this extremely ancient device mysteriously contains within a central "six-lobed rosette" otherwise called the "flower of life." The form of the *Flower of Life*, also known as "Life's Flower," has been known to philosophers, architects, and artists around the world since ancient times. The circle is the most perfect geometric figure, being the same at the beginning as at the end.

Evidence of its importance can be found in almost every major culture around the world. It can be seen in ancient synagogues in Israel, temples within the Forbidden City of China, in the Buddhist temples of India, Japan, carved into the rock in Assyria, in Italian art from the 13th century, and so on.

Figures as prominent as *Leonardo da Vinci* ascribed much significance to the Flower of Life in his work. Da Vinci seemed to have an interest and clearly knew about the symbol-making expressions in his work drawing it in varying forms. His art itself has plenty of patterns embedded within, all of which is Flower of Life derivatives like the *Five Platonic Solids*.

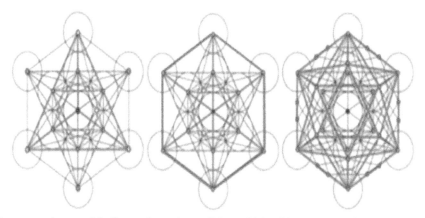

Image above: All five platonic solids within Metatron's Cube. (Public domain.)

From the complete Flower of Life, one can also derive the three-dimensional *Metatron Cube* which holds all the Platonic solids. The Greeks taught that these five solids were the core patterns of physical creation.

"The Flower of Life pattern is a scalable blueprint of the universe." Some claim its purpose is for figuring out everything ranging from the human body to the galaxies extending into the secrets of the universe. It is the blueprint of the universe, containing the basis for the design of every atom, molecular structure, life form, and everything in existence. According to some researchers and scholars, the Seed of Life is a symbol depicting the seven days of creation in which God created life.

Why should anyone pay attention to Metatron? The Bible identifies him as the angel that led the people of Israel through the wilderness after their exodus from Egypt. Metatron's cube is also considered a holy glyph, used to ward off evil spirits in some cultures. It is known by many names throughout the world including a wheel within a wheel the true *Chariot of the Gods*, as described in the Old Testament Book of Ezekiel said to be a "divine light vehicle" used to connect with higher realms. The symmetric form is called a three-dimensional *Star of David*.

It is also the blueprint from which the *Kabbalah Tree of Life* can be derived and has another name which is the *Merkabah*. Author Andrew Monkman writes:

"I believe the complete ancient flower of life is an inter-dimensional tool, a portal, a stargate, a window into what some call the inter space plains."

Image above: Indeed, research reveals the Flower of Life contains a lot of things but how about also a labyrinth hidden inside? *(Public domain.)*

In New Age thought, the Flower of Life as sacred geometry has been provided deep spiritual meaning and forms of enlightenment. It's totally amazing how sacred geometry plays have been found present in the observation of nature, music/sound, and color. These patterns are related to the 7 Chakras of the Hindu faith, the 7 colors of the rainbow, and the 7 notes in music. *DNA stores light*. Both visible and invisible light is part of the electromagnetic spectrum encoded within DNA.

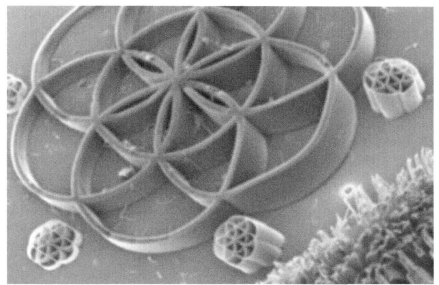

Image above: *Flower of Life structure found to be present within the cross-cut strands of human DNA. (Public domain.)*

Discovering a visual expression of the connection's life weaves through all sentient beings believed to contain a type of *Akashic Record* of basic information of all living things was to say the least enlightening. An additional aspect to the symbolism is to be found in the fact that the geometrical structure of the Flower of Life can also be found in crystallized water being fundamental patterns for everything from atoms to planets and everything in between.

To be able to find this inner/outer connectedness throughout nature is and has been a sign for many for a very long-time along the path providing enlightenment to those who study the symbol and its perfect form. The Seed of Life is formed with seven overlapping circles that create a more singular flower design. To some, this symbolizes the 7 days of creation during which God created life. The discovery of this symbol's meaning has led to its wide use in talismans and magical workings for some believe the amulets and charms behold the magic energy of creation. The purpose of the flower of life is to give life whereby it is sometimes worn by people who want experience help with fertility or need to protect their family.

As taught by followers of Kabbalah the flower of life possesses the vital energies of life contain within available to be utilized by anyone who knows how to be able to tap into. Used often by kabbalists to strengthen the connection to the spiritual light of God drawing in the vibrant living energy from the universe.

The Kabbalistic *Tree of Life* has been theorized to have come from the Flower of Life. As a prominent symbol in the Kabbalah discipline of esoteric Judaism, it is considered by many to be the most powerful pattern of creation in existence as all objects and creatures that are found in the tangible world are believed by some to have emerged from it.

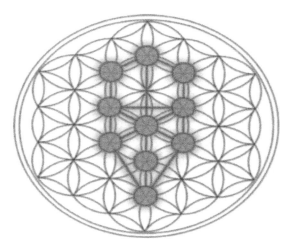

Image above: *Tree of Life symbol found within the Flower of Life. (Public domain.)*

The next 6 circles are identical to the cell division process. Therefore, the *Flower of Life* is seen as a type of model of God's Creation. In these terms, everything can be explained geometrically whether it's animals, people, trees, planets, solar systems, galaxies, etc. Everything in the universe comes out of this single pattern and can be demonstrated by the flower of life.

In Kabbalah tradition, these tools are used to understand the "*map of manifestation*" and nature of God who created the world out of nothingness. The Tree of Life is it seems some sort of "*map of creation*" having spiritual centers when put together form a powerful symbol used to connect to God or to find the union of the divine and the physical self.

The ancient seven-circuit labyrinth (so-called because the path creates seven concentric rings around the center) draws on the mystical quality of the 7, a number of transformations, and vision. The seven circuits can also be seen to represent the days of the week, the chakras, colors, or musical tones. In ancient times, the seven circuits were seen to correspond to the seven visible planets, and a walk in the labyrinth was a cosmic journey through the heavens.

Image above: *The Flower of Life can even be found on the top of the US Dollar bill. (Public domain.)*

In the Kabbalah every circle is aligned with a chakra, called Sephirot, all starting from the original single cell or circle. The next 6 circles are identical to the cell division process. *Each corresponding to a specific chakra being 7 altogether.* Chakra means "wheel" referring to specific energy points in the body thought to be spinning disks of energy corresponding to bundles of nerves, organs, and areas of the energetic body. These circular vortexes of energy are placed in seven different points on the spinal column, and all the seven chakras are connected to the various glands within the body responsible for disturbing the energy. These notable signs clearly show that some labyrinths stand out more than others exposing the fingerprint of a "supernatural genius."

Image above: Under eloquent analysis of the labyrinth, one finds an underlying mathematical machinery of the universe, exposing a purely mental character of universal mathematics, a perception-based programming language comprised of circular wave forms with geometries intersections of light, sound, color, and form inherent to the Flower of Life matrix. *The Flower of Life is the Codex/Rosetta Stone, a universal language. (Public domain.)*

According to some experts on the human experience, the whorls on the fingertips tell of the energy each person has therein. Some are able to read the swirls as energy for meaning. The Navajo state our ancestors were guided by the Reaper, the one who sows each person's life energy.

The Navajo Indians were able to read the whorls for their meaning. The Navajos have a saying about fingerprints:
"The Great Spirit breathes in the breath of life, and the tracks of that breath become our fingerprints."

It is said this is where palm-reading originated.

"The Tao doesn't take sides; it gives birth to both yin and yang. All is welcome, both light and dark." – Lao Tzu

The Twelve Zodiac signs are also said to be found within having the rose in the center which is the calyx: it is the center of the flower which is also the symbol for the opening to the vagina. This calyx is called the "seat and birthplace of God." It is like the Padme of the Great Mantra, which means the lotus.

In searching for our Jerusalem and the peace it brings we try to reach Christ in the inner garden. This difficult journey underlies the symbolism of the labyrinth and being in itself a way having a path—and it is a spiral full of mystery.

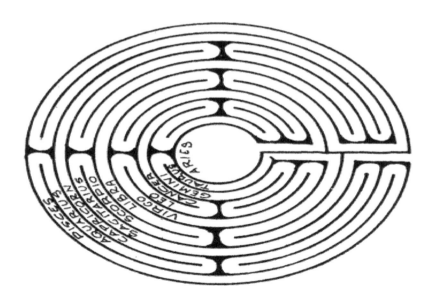

6 THE ANGEL VALLEY LABYRINTH

Throughout Arizona, out in the open or sometimes tucked away, in locations private and public, there are labyrinths where those who choose to walk the mysterious winding paths can clear their minds, let go of the stress life brings hopefully finding a little tranquility along the way.

To date, there are more than 100 labyrinths registered in Arizona, according to the *World-wide Labyrinth Locator* website. 115 miles north of Phoenix sitting on 70 acres nestled in a scrub forest just outside Sedona, Arizona is the *Angel Valley Labyrinth*.

"Angel Valley Labyrinth Practitioners see themselves as *Way-Showers*."

This unique place is built on former ranch property in the red-rock country in the high desert of northern Arizona, said to be a natural environment for healing and self-discovery through a holistic approach aimed at balancing the mind, body, and spirit. Spiritual seekers from all walks of life have made the journey to this place hidden away in the desert to find emotional healing or even make a connection to their guides.

"Angel Valley is a place where all are invited to use nature and the Elementals to discover and to be One's True Natural Divine Self," the builder/founder wrote. "It is about finding and living one's connection with God, with Spirit, with the

Creator, or whatever name one wants to give to the Eternal Source of Life."

Being located next to the city of Sedona, a mecca for spiritual travelers known as the "New Age Capital of the World," nobody blinked an eye when Angel Valley stated its hidden gem was *"a 5th Dimensional Spiritual Oasis and Ascension Portal."* In fact, people seemed to welcome the place.

Image above: The *Angel Valley Labyrinth* outside Sedona Arizona was modeled after the *Chartres Labyrinth. (Public domain.)*

Guided to the property by *Archangel Michael* the retreat was launched sometime in 2002. *"Archangel Michael is one of the Archangels that is assisting mankind to a higher state of awareness and consciousness,"* the builder wrote. *"I made my first conscious connection with Michael in July of 1995 and he has been with me since."* The property was the manifestation of a dream to create an environment where people could visit, live and work that they may feel empowered, be their true self, and to ultimately connected with the divine benevolent self.

"Some labyrinths, especially those connected to churches, are filled with subtle religious symbols."

The resort has been offering a host of New Age and holistic services from its opening called "soul retrieval" and "angel healings," in which a practitioner connects with angels the place states are "strongly connected with and present."
The essence of Angel Valley Sedona is to follow a spiritual path, while doing spiritual work and assisting others in their spiritual growth within the "Six Petal Rose" center, each petal holding the individual energy. Spiritual seekers journey to find guidance, emotional support, and for some, a connection to their guides.

"The Labyrinth is sacred tools to open one's heart, to receive insights, inspiration, and healing, and to connect with one's Higher Self."

According to Angel Valley's website, *"Walking the pattern of the labyrinth induces a shift in your consciousness and in your energy system, consciously or unconsciously."* The labyrinth is further described as a "re-orientation engine" where the walker is the 13th element while in the center, bringing all other levels together into one transcending the consciousness of this reality thus working toward a higher level of consciousness.

"Angel Valley is the premier destination for most spiritual seekers on a spiritual pilgrimage who have been somehow drawn to the sacred land wishing to experience the Divine in an outdoor temple."

When building the Chartres Labyrinth-like structure in 2007, there were 2 main objectives. The first was to build a labyrinth based on the 800-year-old Chartres pattern, and second, for the site to be used as a landing pad for *"Galactic family and friends.*" Shortly after being guided to build the structure through dreams/channeling etc., it was reported by numerous witnesses' UFOs started landing and an extra-terrestrial physically walked among them.

"*We have been informed that over 33 different civilizations that live in other dimensions have landed their ships in the Labyrinth.*"

Of course, these kinds of statements may seem far-fetched to most people. but when taken into account what has been reportedly seen just a few miles away at the famous *Bradshaw Ranch* and other areas in general within the region, these are not outrageous claims. According to some the Angel Valley Chartres, Labyrinth is by far the most naturally empowering and felt vortex in the area. Once inside a person immediately notices something strange has happened and things have somehow changed. The energy stills, it becomes totally quiet, and warmer. It becomes a completely magical experience. "*For Individuals on a journey to be free as their true, natural God-self,*" states the Angel Valley website.

Once you get into the center after walking the walk strange things start to change/happen... The owner/creator of the place says UFO's land here. Always wondered why there were all kinds of signs of Aliens/UFOs pointing towards this place from the Bradshaw Ranch location which is just on the other side of the freeway. The area's extremely high UFO activity along with the story of how the Angel Valley Labyrinth came into being is truly to some out of *The Twilight Zone*, while to others, a key to understanding and discovery.

All the UFOs landing in the region, other strange phenomena taking place, and interdimensional Angels walking around communicating with people informing them to specifically construct elaborate structures said to be used as a gateway/portal just might be a sign something is going on worthy of notice. Often there's a lot of truth to be discovered in myths and legends.

Most the accounts made by those who visit the place are positive even though the skies are alive with the unknown flying around. No matter what, people find the experience magical taking them beyond most of the time.

Entering the serpentine path of the Labyrinth takes a person to their center and back again out into the world giving them wings to fly when done properly. From the micro, into the macro, and back, entering into the Labyrinth is a journey.

"Know ye this Earth is but a portal, guarded by powers unknown to man. Yet, the Dark Lords hide the entrance that leads to the Heaven-born land." Emerald Tablet of Thoth

The blueprint for the Angel Valley Labyrinth construction was based of the Chartres Labyrinth in France. During the Crusades, worshipers on their way to the Holy Land were often preyed upon by bandits who would rob, rape, and even murder pilgrims. These crimes against G-ds people caused the Roman Catholic Church give papal recognition to the problem in 1129. Then a **Catholic** medieval military order whose members combined martial prowess with a monastic life formed to defend the church's holy sites and pilgrims in the Middle East and beyond.

Today we can only look back with wonder and speculation to the group linked to the Holy Grail, the Ark of the Covenant, and even the bloodline of Christ. The truth behind the Knights Templar's secrets rumored to go back to Solomons Temple is one of the most enigmas of all time.

"The significance of the cross of the Knights Templar when it accompanied in battle was of martyrdom: a Christian symbol evoking the sacrifice of Christ on the cross."

In 1099, when the Christian armies took Jerusalem back from Muslim occupation, pilgrims began to arrive in the **Holy Land**. Even after the greatly debated and researched Knights Templar were formed in Jeruselum in

1119 and the army of Christ was employed to protect worshipers, the dangers of traveling to the Holy Land in person still continued along the many miles to the church. The people along the path to the church were often carrying with them offerings that became easy pickings by robbers of which 1000s died.

The church got spiritually medieval ordering the Knights to guard associated building personnel to begin constructing labyrinths.

"The Knights Templar were the first official guardians of not only the house of G-d but the spiritual gateways within."

However, when the Holy Land was lost in the 14th-century public support for the group dwindled causing them to essentially become secretive and go underground leaving a host of legends behind.

For several centuries, the elite Knights Templar group were known as warriors, always ready to fight to defend the land, the church of Christ, the lives of their brothers, and especially their symbol. Of course, the legend of the Knights Templar wouldn't be what it is without the Savior and the rumored to be a race of the fallen Angels taking wisdom and knowledge with them as Atlantis sank.

There are many indirect references to labyrinths being used as a spiritual tool. Legend says that the first design was part of King Solomon's temple and was carried to France by the Templars for the Chartres Labyrinth in France.

The labyrinth at Chartres Cathedral dates back to 1205 when monks used it for contemplative moments to journey within. Its exact origin remains a mystery to this day, but we do know who was enlisted to guard these important places, *The Knights Templar*. Pilgrimage to the Holy City of Jerusalem was made difficult and dangerous by the Crusades. The Church designated seven European cathedrals, mainly in France, to become a type of "Jerusalem" for pilgrims. The labyrinth became the final stage of pilgrimage, serving as a symbolic entry into the "Celestial City of Jerusalem." As the most meaningful esoteric cult object of the twelfth and thirteenth centuries the labyrinth's sacred nature is indicated by the names given it throughout Europe — Chemin de Jérusalem, Iherusalem, and *"City of God."*

This type of labyrinth is to date the most famous being a simple but beautiful six-lobed rosette. Enoch and Elija were both raised to Heaven without death — the only two to be so. They are the two 'witnesses' in Revelation II, and the two extra figures on the Chartre's western central lintel.

Being located next to the city of Sedona, a mecca for spiritual travelers known as the *"New Age Capital of the*

World," nobody blinked an eye when Angel Valley stated its hidden gem was "*a 5th Dimensional Spiritual Oasis and Ascension Portal.*" In fact, people seemed to welcome the place which was modeled after the Chartres labyrinth in France. Guided to the property by *Archangel Michael* the retreat was then soon launched sometime in 2002.

"*Archangel Michael is one of the Archangels that is assisting mankind to a higher state of awareness and consciousness,*" the builder wrote. "*I made my first conscious connection with Michael in July of 1995 and he has been with me since.*"

The historical line of the Angel Valley Labyrinth is pretty clear having its roots connected to the Chartres Labyrinth in France constructed specifically to take people to the Holy Land by the church in the 12th century. Enoch and Elija were both raised to Heaven without death — the only two to be so. They are the two 'witnesses' in Revelation II, and ironically the two extra figures on the Chartre's western central lintel. The six-lobed rosette is to date the most famous labyrinth in the world.

Entrance to the Knights Templar Well not only takes a person spiraling down to the bottom but out to the other side. *Be prepared to go deep into the secrets of not only the Knights Templar but also the labyrinth.*

The Knights Templar Initiation Well

Spiraling deeper into the mystery of the Knights Templar are a pair of wells, called the "Initiation Wells" which spiral down deep within the earth, like inverted towers. The staggering wells were never made to be used to collect water but were instead part of a mysterious initiation ritual within the Knights of Templar traditions.

History states joining the Knights Templar was a highly secretive process. Like any exclusive club or society of the time, new members were required to undergo initiation before being accepted in the ranks. According to legend, Templar initiations at the wells began with candidates entering the initiation well blindfolded where they would descend nine flights of stairs reaching the bottom of one only to walk into a dark labyrinth where they would symbolically and literally find their way up towards the light of the other. If the candidate was able to safely make the journey up and down towers back through the well and into the sunlight, initiates would then be welcomed into the brotherhood.

Many of the rites and rituals of the Knights Templar have been hidden from the masses but are preserved as *Masonic rituals* and are described with great detail in Freemason ritual books. Over the centuries, rumors have swirled about the Templars and the great wealth that they acquired and how they acquired it. In particular, they were thought to have discovered and protected legendary treasures. Although the Order was dissolved by the Church and vilified by all Western monarchies in the 14th century, the Knights Templar has survived to this day in many forms even after being burned alive and accused of worshiping Baphomet.

The half-human and half-animal, male and female, good and evil, of the figure of Baphomet, who in depictions displays a host of symbolism of not only being a winged figure who points to the "above and below" but also the medical Caduceus. To the average person these symbols may seem demonic in nature, but nonetheless, point directly towards conveying a specific message to those who have eyes to see. "It's obvious from the symbolism, the Knights Templars knew about the Angel who traveled from the heavens above into the earth below."

The name *Baphomet* appeared in trial transcripts for the Inquisition of the Knights Templar in 1307. There in black and white in the trial depositions, one has to address perhaps the most shocking of all, however, was the testimony involving a decapitated bearded head that was worshiped taking us even further down the mysterious initiation rite hole of the secret order.

Some scholars have claimed the name of Baphomet was an Old French corruption of the name "Mohammed." 'Riding the Goat' was a common phrase that meant becoming a Freemason in the early 20th century. "*Who is this goat who has access to the above and below, and why was it found within the Knights Templar tale and Freemasonry?"*

To this day the image can be found worshiped inside churches.

The first Gnostic in this world was blessed Mercurius. As the messenger of the G'ds, according to legend he has the ability to travel from heaven to hell, and back again. This symbolically reveals that Hermes is a neutral force, and being a neutral force, he has the capability to investigate all truths. For he can filter through all the chaos and lies, separating the wheat from the chaff, which gives him the intelligence, and strength to find the truth in all things." ~ Paul Francis Young

Unmasking the synagogue of Satan has never been an easy quest for a Christian, however, the journey is without question necessary for a Knight who went to great lengths to protect the Holy Land on all fronts.

"It must be duly noted that despite the many accusations brought out about the Knights Templar were years later dismissed."

There are perhaps other signs available that may point to where the meaning of "*As above, so Below*" originated. The term as above, so below is linked to *King Solomon* the son of David. The phrase and symbol speak for themselves volumes of information. *Give the King a shave and one finds the cross bound within the Star of David.* Commonly associated with Judaism the Star of David is and the people.

The expression as above, so below was first seen on the Emerald Tablet of Hermes Trismegistus, hence its close ties to Hermeticism.

Choose the path

The natural progression of the labyrinth on earth begins at the base of Mount Hermon where the Watchers Angels of God descended. At the base, there is the site in Hebrew called Gilgal Refā'īm or Galgal Refā'īm, "Wheel of Spirits" or "Wheel of Ghosts" as Refa'im means "ghosts" or "spirits" found in the first collum. Christ, a firstborn that all belong to the Lord according to biblical text, visited the place with his disciples shortly before being crucified.

After Christ's crucifixion appears the next generation of the labyrinth in another yet similar form found in Jewish mysticism the middle pillar found in the second row below with corresponding imagery for those who understand symbolism.

The Apotheosis of Washington is another example of the gateways giving credit to the older ones but is modern and pagan something warned about in ancient texts. Choosing the right path is critical. There's man's way which comes at a cost and then what God already gave instilled inside naturally...

One keeps you grounded in nature to Mother Earth, the other to above and below, and the last above only of the Pagan Gods or in other words the powers and principalities... (We see today the result of allowing all the different gods into the US system and what happens.)

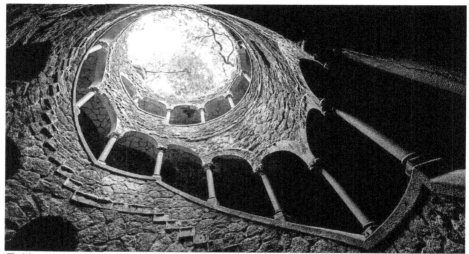

Exiting the Knights Templar Initiation Well back up into the light.

The Shining Ones

Hang around the Angel Valley retreat vicinity long enough and a person is bound to see something fly through the sky. The idea of supernatural portals, doorways, and secret openings to other dimensions has existed for a very long time. The American Indians, Assyrians, Egyptians, Greeks, the Hindus, Sumerians, and virtually all other civilizations wrote about it. Beings of super intelligence sometimes referred to as "gods" descend through openings of the sky to the earth to interact with this planet's creatures.

The concept that gateways between our world and other dimensions exist or can be created actually is an ancient one which through an entity can pass. According to myths/legends it's been happening since the dawn of time, which has been recorded in the history, holy books, and mythos of every great civilization. Rabbinical authorities including Septuagint translators understood it.

Personally the bottom line rests in the fact one can take the long, drawn-out route by waiting for something to happen on their own, or get right down to business by hiring a professional who knows where the events are most likely to be taking place. There are many types of UFO sightings in the Sedona/Verde Valley region ranging from metallic craft to the luminous specifically the "orbs."

Angels/Orbs seem to be the most dominant supernatural sightings taking place near the labyrinth. The creator/owner as well as many others have all stated these types of paranormal events happen on a regular basis. Who and what these craft/beings truly are has been a matter of question for some time, however, perhaps there's mention of them further in the ancient texts matching the luminous characteristics.

From myths and legends, the true identity of the "Shining Ones" is considered to be one of the greatest secrets ever kept from humanity. Examinations of sacred ancient texts reveal this amazing race of beings created mankind and walked among humans and were of great importance to ancient civilizations worldwide. The Shining Ones have appeared in many myths and cultures by different names and descriptions always as gods or creational forces of light. The most realistic definition of these beings is that they were highly intelligent extraterrestrial beings who ultimately creating animals and mankind. The Egyptian Book of the Dead speaks of these beings in Chapter 134 - 14/17 - "The Gods" it clearly states:

"Behold, O ye shining ones, ye men and gods, ye damned ones, when ye behold Osiris Ani, triumphant like unto Horus and adored by reason of the ureret crown, fall ye down upon your faces; for Osiris Ani is victorious over his foes in the heavens above and on the earth beneath, in the presence of the godlike rulers. Of all the gods and goddesses."

This is the tale of the Watchers was an esoteric group of beings mentioned and revered by many cultures calling them Elohim (Ancient Hebrews called them Elohim much like the ancient Sumerians, who viewed them as the owners of mankind and its watchers) or Shining Ones were considered to be most powerful beings ever to exist, the ones who forged the human body and soul and to have walked with mankind in ages long forgotten. Famous masonic historian General Albert Pike specifically noted in Morals and Dogma, the Elohim/Watchers were seen as the "hosts of heaven" traveling between worlds. Their leader, Yahweh Elohim can be translated as Leader of the Shining Ones.

According to some researchers, even the Native American shamans tell of the Bak'Ti gods, which the term translates to Shining Ones who descended on Earth millions of years ago establishing a base where they engineered mankind. Early records of *The Shining Ones* can be found in 5 basic sources:

1: Sumerian tablets from the library in Nippur where they are called by the name Annunaki (Anannage)
2: In Bible, Book of Genesis, Numbers, Deuteronomy, where the name of Nephilim was given to them
3: Writings in Greece that can be accounted to Babylonian priest Berossus
4: The Book of Enoch, where they are mentioned by the name of Angels, Watchers, Nephilim
5: Book of Jubilees

The Bible makes reference to the Shining Ones as the Watchers appearing to Moses's father Amram:

"And there appeared two men very tall, such as I have never seen on earth. And their faces shone like the sun, and their eyes were like burning lamps, and fire forth from their lips. Their dress had the appearance of feathers… [purple], their wings were brighter than gold, their hands whiter than snow. They stood at the head of my bed and called by my name."

Furthermore, ancient Hebrew scripture tells of the birth of Noah being a progeny of the Shining Ones stating:

"And after some days my son, Methuselah, took a wife from his son Lamech, and she became pregnant by him and bore him a son. And his body was white as snow and red as a rose; the hair of his head as white as wool and his edema [long curly hair] beautiful; and as for his eyes, when he opened them, the whole house glowed like the sun.

And his father, Lamech was afraid of him and fled and went to Methuselah his father; and he said to him "I have begotten a strange son. He is not like an (ordinary) human being but he looks like the children of the angels of heaven to me, his form is different and he is not like us. It does not seem to me that he is of me, but of the angels."

According to Sumerian creation stories, Angels were known under the name of Anunnaki or Anannage (great sons of Anu), founders of their culture. A (Sumerian) was the chief God of Sun and Sky, and his name literally means *"The Shining One."* According to this, the Anunnaki were, *"Suns of the Shining One"* or *"Suns of Light."* The same researchers concluded there is furthermore evidence of a connection with the Shining Ones in Sumerian tablets and Bible stating:

"Ninlil or Ninkharsag 'Lady of Kharsag,' wife of Enlil, asks the council of seven to create Eden (E-din) or heavenly garden. For Sumerians, E-din was an 'abode of rightful ones.' This is the same heavenly garden that also can be found in the Bible. The tree of life and knowledge in the biblical garden alludes to the secrets of the Shining Ones. It can be associated with the 'tree' of seven chakras, the 'tree' which lead the Shining One into 'heaven.' This tree later became the 'tree of life in the esoteric system of Qabalah. Number seven has cosmologically wide significance, and the council of seven is the same as seven archangels or seven messengers from the Bible, which came from the heavens. Sumerians built their towers or Ziggurats with seven levels. It was said that the Shining deities resided at the top of Ziggurat – the 'Great House' or Ekur."

The Hebrew myth is very similar to the one found in the Sumerian "Epic of Gilgamesh" furthermore linking with the Book of Genesis ends with the story of the Tower of Babel (Babylon), ironically at that time situated in the region of the Sumerian empire. To this end, the story in the Bible suggests "secret knowledge" was connected with the Shining Ones initially brought in Babylon and then transferred from there.

Its true most of the ancient texts have been doctored over the years to paint a specific viewpoint to keep the people in line with the powers that be desired but have nevertheless left a window open for viewing here and there. No doubt there have been powerful forces at work behind the scenes controlling what is able to be presented and taken in the minds of humanity. It has been the Church for the most part who has influenced and carefully erased any proof of the Shining One's existence from history.

The Book of Enoch is a perfect example and is said to hold vital information related to the identity of the Shining Ones, which is why according to some the book was removed from the Bible and then hidden away. The scribe Enoch taught by the Shining Ones, was employed after that as a messenger or intermediate between the Shining Ones and the "Ones who fell". The fallen ones decided to leave their "divinity" to live amongst the people. This book is not included in canonical books today, and most of the Christian churches consider it as pseudepigrapha. However, the Ethiopian Orthodox Church regards it to be canonical to this day. *The biggest question is why has the truth about these beings been kept hidden from humanity on such a massive scale?* One researcher and author remarked:

"The slight thought of such beings to exist and govern our lives would shatter the very foundations of the all-ruling Church, so its reign continues as long as no other disputant questions the Church's firm grasp over the entire world. Because of this, we have very little information about the Shining Ones' identity."

In all of the above cultures, there are records of special groups representing the elite of the Shining Ones who have remained powerful groups that experienced the enlightenment of these beings. In Sumeria, is the Egregore or Watchers and many other epithets which were given to them. From all of these then we can conclude that they also were the Shining Ones. The Shining Ones are also found in the Bible and are considered to be "Angels of God." The Essenes were the Hebrew sect for which it was said to stand behind the writings of the Dead Sea Scrolls. The name "Essenes" comes from Hebrew meaning "preserver" or "guardian." They also were called Watchers, "Sons of Light" and "Servants of God."

Research indicates it has been the Church who has tried to erase this almost forgotten race from history, nevertheless, the bright legacy of the Shining Ones lives on, found captured on local cameras and etched into the local petroglyph walls along with the many myths and legends. There is no question these beings have existed in the past according to numerous historical texts and local legends and are said to be returning again.

There has been some research into these mysterious beings over the years resulting in some revealing information shining through the clouds of deception. The Shining Ones: The World's Most Powerful Secret Society Revealed by Philip Gardiner states:

"The story of The Shining Ones is the real history of mankind. Every twist and turn on the pathway of human evolution was put there deliberately by this secret priesthood for a mysterious and extremely long-term goal. On our journey to uncover the Shining Ones we will learn that history, as we know it, is a lie. History is, as Justice Holmes said, 'what the people who won say it is.' It has been warped over vast periods of time to fit with each generation's idea of what is fact and what is truth. Our belief systems, whether religious, scientific, or political, have been manipulated by a secret and deadly group of individuals who have a history going back thousands of years. They have a name, they

have a power base and they have a secret, locked away within their initiated few, which has major implications for the future of mankind. We will discover the secret and reveal it. Once we decipher the Shining Ones' clues, we will see how the mysteries of the ancient and not so ancient world can now be solved, from megalithic standing stones, the Holy Grail, and alchemy to the truth behind religion and our present political systems. We must forget the false interpretations of myth and religion we have heard so many times, and know them for what they really are: the secret language of the Shining Ones."

A person can find the Shining Ones in other religions and areas as well as Hinduism, Buddhism, Jainism that are predominated East. Records indicate for thousands of years; these Shining Ones worshiped the "inner light inside themselves like it was Sun itself" and this idea of enlightenment they carried with themselves wherever they went. Since recorded history and even before these beings have appeared all over the world leaving very little room to doubt what they are.

Found by the famous paranormal Bradshaw Ranch in the Secret Canyon wilderness are petroglyph images protected by the US government which clearly show ancient people standing in front of and speaking to "Shining Ones" or "Suns" something ironically found in the region flying around in modern times.

Additionally, there were no local conventional churches known of today who were back in the area when the Yavapai people emerged from Montezuma Well traveling somewhere on Mingus mountain and had relations with a "Shining One" thus giving birth to the legend of the *"Yavapai: People of the Sun"* and ultimately the *"The Verde Valley Giant"* the result of the mixing of humans with Shining Ones.

Mingus Mountain next to Jerome, Arizona.

Take into account what was witnessed and captured on camera in the sky where clearly what appear to be shining ones can be seen descending onto Mingus Mountain the evidence is pretty clear and bright. Other legends of Montezuma Well have the strange place as being the home of the god Quetzalcoatl was, as the name indicates, a feathered serpent-like a dragon who was a boundary-maker (and transgressor) between earth (going into the underworld) and sky (heavens) above. Quetzalcoatl was a creator deity having contributed essentially to the creation of Mankind.

Legend says Quetzalcoatl mouth is viewed as a wormhole, a place for arrival and departure of spirit beings portrayed as having a ladder descend from the sky by the Mayas. *Isn't it a little odd and strange there is a false bottom to the well the depths of which have yet to be explored and we have this extraordinary legend of a being who can descend from the heavens straight on into the depths of the underworld?* There are indeed depths and legends found in *"The Very Mysterious Montezuma Well"* worthy of notice connected to this figure.

The Mesoamerican Plumed (or Feathered) Serpent legend/myth has fascinated humanity for quite some time. This god was believed to bring good tidings and even civilization itself to humankind. The preeminent role in ancient times of the being among the Aztecs and Toltecs is evident from the fact that not only were whole civilizations with temples constructed around but whole cities were built as centers of worship including pyramid structures the likes of which are ironically found close by locally at Tuzigoot National Monument. Tuzigoot National Monument is a pyramid.

The connections between these myths/legends of the gods, the powers they possessed, and where they originated from are undeniable. Not only were these beings said to be shapeshifters giving rise to the many Skinwalker/Bigfoot and other similar myths/legends but also could walk among humans looking as one as well. Some historians claim a few of these beings required human sacrifice.

Despite the attempts to control all the information in the world about these beings of light, they keep showing up doing their things which according to some have been directing the course of humanity from the beginning. Nevertheless, for those who can't stomach all the misleading lies, the quest for truth remains paramount leading as a way to discovery. One researcher perhaps stated it best about the purpose behind the quest saying:

"We hope that the ones who read this will ask themselves, how well do they know the world in which we all live in, about the truth that actually happened in the past and the one the history tells us. We hope you will all ask yourselves about the world in which we live today, who is really pulling all the strings and what is their connection with all past events and why some things are constantly being kept hidden from us. We hope this will provoke people to question what they have been taught and to see what we take for granted. This is because in these times we constantly have new facts emerging from the darkness which are showing us that there is a difference between what we know and what is just now coming out to the light."

Further research has shown connections with these Shining Ones and the "Phoenix" and the city "Phoenix," the "Phoenix Lights," on the back of the dollar bill is the "Phoenix" who is also at the United Nations presiding over in a painting is the "Phoenix." The Angels, Seraphim, are described as bright as the sun, a "Phoenix" enflamed... Make no question about it these beings have been coming and going for some time as is clearly shown in history and on the walls of the surrounding area ancient petroglyphs.

The word phoenix originates in ancient Egypt, and Phoenicia is where, according to the book of Enoch, the fallen angels first descended upon Mount Hermon. From there some claim (Wayne Steiger) the Land of the Serpent Gods, America, became the home of this character. When President Bush stated, "And an angel still rides in the whirlwind and directs this storm" he was speaking the literal truth! Presiding over the United Nations... The Phoenix AKA "The Shining One" is also found on the crest of other nations... Rome, Nazis, Russia, and so on...

In some of the witch lores of Italy, the Watchers are referred to in an old Strega myth (recounted in Leland's Aradia - Gospel of the Witches, published in 1890). In these legends, we find the words:
"Then Diana went to the fathers of the Beginning, to the mothers, the spirits who were before the first spirits."

These spirits are the Grigori, also known in some traditions as "The Old Ones" an ancient race that has evolved beyond the need for a physical form. In some legends, the Watchers were said to have originally come from the stars. It may even be possible that the Watchers have a connection with ancient Egypt. In the Mystery Teachings of Egypt, one of the password phrases to gain access to the temple was:

"*Though I am a child of the earth, my Race is of the stars.*"

The Grigori (from Greek "The Watchers") are a group of fallen angels described in biblical apocrypha, dispatched to earth to watch over the people as "Watchers" or

"Sentinels" who are mentioned alongside the "holy ones" in the Book of Daniel in the bible. In some witchcraft and Wiccan systems, the Watchers are beings who guard the known sometimes in the past stone portals said to be able to link worlds together. These supernatural guardians maintain the portals to other realms, but also protectors of the ritual circle.

Ruled over by four great Watchers known as Michael, Gabriel, Raphael, and Auriel. In the Apocryphal Books of Enoch and Jubilees, the Watchers were sent to Earth to teach law and justice to humankind.

The biblical *Tree of Life* in the garden alludes to secrets of the Shining Ones associated with the "tree" of seven chakras, the "tree" which leads the Shining One into adobe of the gods, "heaven."

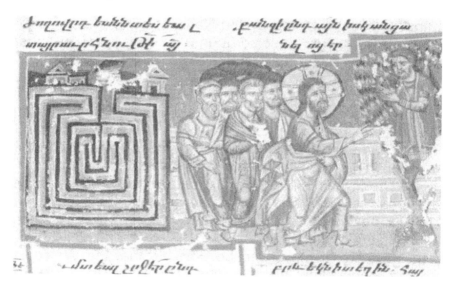

Christs Labyrinth

Author and Ancient Aliens show contributor William Henry has given seminars about Christ becoming a *Seraphim Angel* who could travel around in a rainbow light body. That being said perhaps the legends of the Yavapai

People being found with crosses on their foreheads by the Spanish looking for gold is a sign.

Throughout history there are tales of a mysterious person who walked America in ancient times teaching people who some claim was Christ. These accounts are even part of a religion like in the *Book of Mormon.* For centuries people have been reportedly seeing and speaking with this person who mysteriously appears out of nowhere. To find his presents in the Sedona/Verde Valley region throughout history is something to consider. The oral histories concerning the pale God who visited native American tribes all over the Americas backs up the New Testament of the East, with the Christian Indian legends of the West.

There is no question with all the records left behind two thousand years ago a mysterious white man walked from tribe to tribe among the American Nations who spoke many languages, healed the sick, even raised the dead according to some, and taught in the same words of Christ proof that the Savior came not only to one continent, but to the world.

"In Chartres, scholars believe that the monks created the labyrinth in 1205 to represent the human path from sin to redemption."

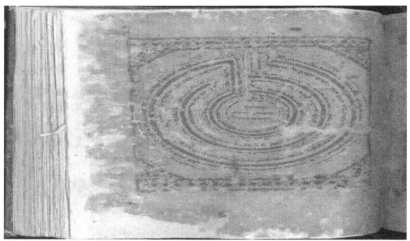

The labyrinth is found in Hebrew texts. The oldest known Jericho labyrinth with the same alignment as in the Taj Torah can be seen on a page of a Hebrew Old Testament which was completed by Josef von Xanten in 1294.

Without question someone went to a lot of trouble to build the labyrinth in France housing the veil of Mary and so on ultimately making it *"Christ's Labyrinth."* Then others followed the same intricate path like what is found at the Angel Valley Labyrinth.

If the labyrinth was built for people who could not make the journey to the *Holy Land* in person, then how is it a person is able to benefit from walking into one? *What does entering the labyrinth have to do with the Holy Land? Why do some labyrinth contain the "Flower of Life" and other mysteries like Metatron Cube and others not so?*

There is another place holding perhaps another clue to the mystery containing some more connections. Alatri is a small town in Lazio, south of Rome. Alatri was the city of the Templars. A church with an adjoining cloister, dating from the thirteenth century, is dedicated to *St. Francis of Assisi*. St Francis is a very interesting person who was said to speak to Angels including Christ himself.

There is a shrine dedicated to the saint Sedona Chapel of the Holy Cross. The church of St. Francis of Assisi dates from the 13th century completely identical to the one that decorates the floor of the nave of the cathedral of Chartres, the "Cathedral of the Mystery" par excellence, in France.

According to Professor *Graziella Frezza* from the *Ministry of Cultural Heritage* of the Italian Republic, the Alatri frescos and its the Knights Templars who are considered the likely authors of the fresco of "*Christ in the Labyrinth*."

In 1996 a tunnel was discovered beneath the church, with a number of fresco paintings on its walls, including spirals, circles, plants, flowers of life and a unique depiction of "Christ in Glory" at the center of a large labyrinth.

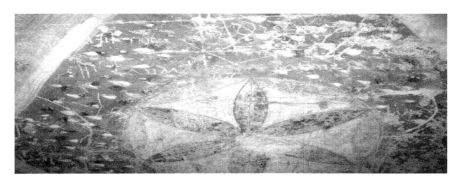

The authors are not known but the study of the other decorations ("Flowers of Life", "Triple Circumferences", "Spirals", "Stars" etc.) tends to attribute it to the Order of the "Pauperes Commilitiones Christi Templique Salomonici," better known as *Knights Templar*.

In his left-hand Christ is holding the Holy Book, while his right hand points towards the entrance of the labyrinth. The message seems clear: it's an invitation to go the road inwards – the inner pilgrimage – that in the end leads to knowledge of the sacred, guarded and transferred by Christ himself. Christ has a halo and holds a book with the left hand (placed almost in correspondence with the heart) while the right hand, whose fingers are bent in the sign of blessing, indicates the entrance (or exit) of the labyrinth. "Christ in the Labyrinth"

You enter coming from where the sun sets, from the darkness, and you start in the direction in which it rises, towards the Light. In this labyrinth there is no fear of taking the wrong path, of confusing oneself, those who face it have only two possibilities: follow its twists and turns until the end, confident that it will reach the center (where, in this case, Christ in person awaits him) or turn around. The confident abandonment to the path of the "unicursal" labyrinth bears witness to a profession of faith, based on total and serene abandonment to a Higher Will.

It has been suggested that the places with the same labyrinths the Alatri-Chartres type indicate the stages of a journey or pilgrimage or spiritual initiation for the person who reunites with *God* and therefore with himself. The one who enters the labyrinth is on the way to its final destination or the center and core of its being representing the alchemy of the soul on its journey towards the Divine.

In an age when many people are looking beyond the church pulpit for spiritual experience, many have rediscovered the labyrinth as a path to prayer and introspection. The labyrinth is a tool to unlock the mystery of our soul's calling. More than just a walk in the woods Labyrinths are almost magical, in a sense, because of their extraordinary powers being more about the journey, at least as much as the destination.

Guardians of the Gateways (Knights Templar)

During the Crusades, worshipers on their way to the Holy Land were often preyed upon by bandits who would rob, rape, and even murder pilgrims. These crimes against G-ds people caused the Roman Catholic Church give papal recognition to the problem in 1129. Then a Catholic medieval military order whose members combined martial prowess with a monastic life formed to defend the church's holy sites and pilgrims in the Middle East and beyond.

Even after the Knights Templar were formed and the army was employed to protect worshipers the dangers of traveling to the Holy Land in person still continued along the many miles to the church. The church got spiritually medieval ordering the Knights to guard and associated building personnel to begin constructing labyrinths.

The labyrinth at Chartres Cathedral dates back to 1205 when monks used it for contemplative moments to journey within. Its exact origin remains a mystery to this day, but we do know who was enlisted to guard these important places, "The Knights Templar." Pilgrimage to the Holy City of

Jerusalem was made difficult and dangerous by the Crusades. The Church designated seven European cathedrals, mainly in France, to become a type of "Jerusalem" for pilgrims. The labyrinth became the final stage of pilgrimage, serving as a symbolic entry into the "Celestial City of Jerusalem." As the most meaningful esoteric cult object of the twelfth and thirteenth centuries the labyrinth's sacred nature is indicated by the names given it throughout Europe—Chemin de Jérusalem, Iherusalem, and "City of God."

7 NEXT TO THE BRADSHAW RANCH

Across the freeway on Arizona State Route 89A outside Sedona directly across from the phenomenal Angel Valley Labyrinth is the *Bradshaw Ranch* approximately 10 miles away. The area is famous for its strange UFO and other supernatural sightings down a long, rough, dirt road winding through the desert until it was purchased by the United States Congress. Congress does not normally buy ranches, however, for some special reason they felt the need to snatch up the place after reports of strange anomalies started to plague the Bradshaw Family.

"The Bradshaw's and the owners of the Angel Valley Labyrinth all attest to there being intergalactic portals in the region through which UFOs, ETs, and other beings freely travel through on a regular basis."

The famous ranch is all padlocked now with a sign prohibiting entry. The rumor is that it was confiscated by the U.S. Government in May of 2003 for $3.5 million dollars because it housed one of the most powerful inter-dimensional portals on the planet. Visitors are not allowed in the National Forest region at night, but several tour operators will take you there and stay until dusk if you were to pay them enough money. According to eyewitness accounts, it's the last hour of twilight when many of these strange phenomena takes place having been captured numerous times on film attracting a considerable amount of attention. (*What remains unexplained is why the federal agency has forbidden access to the taxpaying public "who paid for the land" since May 10, 2003*.) Most researchers and people would find these kinds of connections rather perplexing but they should in themselves speak for themselves. The ranch continues to attract international recognition as a paranormal hotspot through various television programs, books, tours, and other adventures.

The ranch got its name when Hollywood stuntman *Bob Bradshaw* acquired the 140-acre ranch in 1960 for $200 an acre. At that time, all that remained of the original homestead was an old adobe house believed to be the oldest pioneer structure in the area. When he wasn't working in the movies, Bradshaw turned the property into a working ranch and movie set which served as the primary location for many movies, two television series, and lots of commercials. In total, over fifty full-length motion pictures were shot in the area.

After the purchase of the Bradshaw Ranch by the US Government people started to get a sense there was a strong military presence in the area afterward. Any suspicions before the event were made even more formidable. Once the land was obtained the area was immediately posted prohibiting anyone from entering onto the land, and guards for some odd reason began to turn visitors away.

The Sedona Red Rock News was the first to report Congress wanted the Bradshaw Ranch. (Public domain.)

The locals who live in the area say that the government is covering up doorways found to exist in the area where inter-dimensional entities are said to be coming through a wide-open dimensional corridor. While some may doubt, dimensional corridors are held by physicists to be possible. In fact, the Bible describes gates and doors beyond which both good and evil intelligence exists and that, at times, come through these doorways into our reality.

No other region in the continental United States compares when it comes to UFOs. According to UFO Digest, the Bradshaw Ranch *"has seen more paranormal activity in recent years than perhaps any other US location,"* so much so, it appears to have attracted the attention of the US Federal Government who not only bought the land but then prohibited public access to.

It has been reported bizarre and strange paranormal activity was first described by the Bradshaw's themselves. Linda Bradshaw described flying *"Balls of Light"* witnessing a host of strange activity and phenomena which ultimately lead her to conclude the site had become an active "inter-dimensional portal." Linda herself wrote that while living on-site one evening she was walking on the property:

"Before my eyes, a huge and brilliant light appeared in the sky above me. I did not see anything but the light itself and it remained there for only a few seconds."

On another evening after the first sighting a now wiser and with camera in hand, she observed the light balls in the sky again in the same spot:

"I only had time to click the shutter twice, when the light instantly closed, leaving me to question whether it had been real."

After living on the ranch for two years, Linda Bradshaw observed:

"I believe these openings have always been on our plane and they've perhaps been the portals to allow others in, but if one were to ask my opinion of my experiences regarding this magical place, I would say that not only are they being allowed in, but they are coming in great numbers. I would

also love to say that only compassionate beings of light are scooting through these portals, but this does not always seem to be the case. I have come face to face with a few decidedly nasty beings."

Linda Bradshaw went on to co-author a book, *"Merging Dimensions,"* which details her many strange experiences on the Ranch – including preponderance for Orbs of many colors to float around her. She describes these and Comet like objects which hovered off the ground and shot energy past her. As word of these incidents grew, the homestead was soon featured on a paranormal TV show called "Sightings" in 1992.

The fact there are television shows who capture video of the Orbs flying around while on location at the Bradshaw Ranch numerous times on separate occasions is startling. *These reports seem to match what people were also seeing and reporting occurring at the Angel Valley Labyrinth just a short distance away.*

After the purchase of the Bradshaw Ranch by the US Government people really started to get a sense there was a strong military presence in the area afterward. Any suspicions before the event were made even more formidable. Then in a bold move the US Government out of nowhere turned over the famous ranch to *Northern Arizona University.* People really don't know what to call the place now.

"All the UFO activity in the area makes the Angel Valley Labyrinth unlike any other in the world."

People have been visiting Sedona for Millennia. Over half of the near 4+ million annual visitors to Sedona come in search of a spiritual experience. It is Arizona's second most popular tourist attraction after the Grand Canyon. *Is Sedona sacred?* Look at Courthouse Rock, next to Bell Rock, and you find it is a red rock version of the *Devil's Tower,* which featured so prominently in Close Encounters of the Third

Kind. Devil's Tower was a sacred site to the Native Americans of the region.

Some researchers contend Sedona's spiritual heritage actually goes back for millennia. The Spring 2015 Edition of the Visitor's Guide published by the Sedona Red Rock News, states that archeologists believe the ancient Sinagua/Anasazi people may have held Sedona as sacred ground in the same way people do today, sense their ruins ring Sedona in the Verde Valley area. It is thought these people of the distant past lived on the outskirts and traveled into the red rock area to be part of a sacred ceremony.

Found throughout the Sedona region are dwellings at places like Montezuma Castle National Monuments, Montezuma Well National Monuments, and Tuzigoot National Monuments, which reflect the area in ancient times was indeed a vibrant community.

Montezuma Well is about twenty minutes by car from Sedona. The Well has a number of cliff dwellings and is something of a geological enigma – or, at least, an anomaly. It produces vast and consistent qualities of warm water, which rises from somewhere deep underground. Scientists have not yet discovered the origin of the consistently warm water. It is nevertheless clear that the Yavapai were aware of this enigmatic resurgence, and have linked it with their creation mythology. As the Yavapai believe – like e.g., the Hopi – that we live in the Fourth World, for them, the Third World, is literally our "underworld", and we emerged from under the earth into this Fourth World. Hence why, no doubt, Montezuma Well is used as a place of emergence.

Can Sedona and the surrounding area really be so sacred? Look at Courthouse Rock, next to Bell Rock, and you find it a small red rock version of the *Devil's Tower*, which featured so prominently in *Close Encounters of the Third Kind*. Devil's Tower was a sacred site to the Native Americans of the region. Some believe Devil's Tower is the stump of an ancient tree that was cut off separating heaven from earth.

For the Hopi, the "Red City" was a great cultural and religious center from a previous area. The Native Americans traveled from there, towards the Mesas which meant for them a return to the world of spirit, a pilgrimage, a vision quest to a site where they would commune with their ancestral spirits.

We should perhaps ask whether the cliff dwellings of Boynton Canyon, Montezuma Well (and Castle), and the settlement of Tuzigoot really are "just" settlements, or whether they are instead sacred structures used for pilgrims who came here, seeking inspiration, guidance, or initiation. The American Indian elders who reside in the area state the Sedona/Verde Valley has "always been a sacred holy place" often referred to as "*God's land.*"

The Sedona/Verde Valley area is without a doubt one of the most mystical and magical places on earth. People from all walks of life throughout the world for millennia have made the journey to this breathtaking and unforgettable land. No question Sedona's a stunner, but it's intensely spiritual as well – some even say sacred. Sedona is an Arizona desert oasis a short distance from Flagstaff that's surrounded by beautiful red-rock buttes, steep canyon walls, and pine forests. The area is noted for its mild climate and vibrant arts community. Sedona is also dense with New Age shops, spas, and art galleries.

Many New Age types believe that this area is the center of vortexes (not 'vortices' here in Sedona) that radiate the Earth's power, and Sedona's combination of scenic beauty and mysticism draws throngs of tourists year-round. For such a small town there sure has been a remarkable array of famous people who have lived at and visited Sedona's mysteries over the years.

"With over 4+ million visitors a year to the region one can't but wonder what has attracted so many people to visit the Sedona area."

It has been said Sedona's main attraction is the area's array of red sandstone formations. These formations appear to glow in brilliant red and orange when illuminated by the rising or setting sun. The red rocks form a popular backdrop for many activities, ranging from spiritual pursuits at famous vortex locations to the hundreds of hiking and mountain biking trails.

The Land Preservation Task Force

The Land Preservation Task Force founded in 1996 decided they needed outside help to acquire some of the unique and significant lands in the Sedona area to donate to the US Forest Service. Through various, some say where underhanded means using such excuses as eminent domain referring to the power of the government to take private property and convert it into public use the group acquired the following:

Thompson Original Homestead of 15.5 acres in Munds Canyon, a side canyon to Oak Creek Canyon and source of one of the mainsprings feeding Oak Creek. Acquired 8/98 for $1.1 million.

Cleeves Property, a parcel of approximately 110 acres at the end of the road just past Honanki Ruin in the Red Cliffs area of Yavapai County, 18 miles northwest of Sedona. Acquired 3/99 for $2.3 million.

Woo Ranch, a 160-acre parcel in the Red Cliffs area, adjacent to Palatki Ruin about 10 miles northwest of Sedona. Acquired 8/00 for $6.9 million.

Smyrnis property, a 25-acre parcel adjacent to Cleeves Property northwest of Sedona. Acquired 8/00 for $.5 million.

Bradshaw Ranch, a 90-acre parcel in the area of Red Canyon northwest of Sedona. Acquired 4/01 for $3.5 million.

Hancock Ranch, an 88-acre ranch and the residence of area pioneer rancher Mary Hancock, before her death at age 96. Acquired 5/04 for $3.95 million.

Thomas Point, a rugged 25-acre parcel adjacent to Highway 89A in beautiful Oak Creek Canyon. Acquired 6/05 for $0.6 million.

These properties were reported transferred to Coconino National Forest to further protect the ecosystems of the Sedona/Oak Creek area, archaeological sites, scenic vistas, and historic homesteads between 1998-2005.

The Hancock Ranch was one of the last large private parcels in Sedona's Red Rock area to become taken over by the US government who somehow again got the estimated value of 90+ million ranches to be sold for under 3.95 million something also done to the Bradshaw Ranch which is ironically in the same region. It was clear someone wanted the land adjacent to the Honanki Heritage Site, one of the largest cliff dwellings in Coconino National Forest and the site of ancient petroglyph cave art, as well as more.

"The value comes with preserving the character of the land and preventing it from future development," said Judy Adams, who is with the Forest Service and who had involvement with the land purchase. "The Hancock Ranch was one of the high-priority lands we wanted to acquire." Funding for the project came from the federal Land and Water Conservation Fund with the strong support of U.S. Sen. Jon Kyl and U.S. Rep. Bob Stump.

Newspapers and other sources reported the Hancock Ranch was turned over without a fight but this isn't completely true. There were people close to the family who stated there was a lot of pressure from officials and locals to acquire the place just like there was at the Bradshaw Ranch.

Rumor was at the time the pressure had its toll as well as what was happening at the ranch. The fact the US Government as well as other groups have purchased all the land up around the area should be a great indication something is worth all the effort. However, some claim all the land buy up is due to the impact human activities would have on forest lands especially in the Sedona region anticipating increased population and changes in tourism. However, the next player on stage with its cross pointing to the sky not far away may be pointing at something else altogether as to why all the interest in the region.

NBC news did a story airing nationally about movies made in Sedona, AZ in 1996. In the video, you hear Bob Bradshaw state something odd relating to it was the US Forest Service who bought up all the land through various means only to start "trading off the hills" ultimately to turn what was once called "Gods Land," a place made for movies, into a booming housing development the area has become today full of tourist and tours. According to Bob Bradshaw, there was hardly a home in the region until the US Forest Service and Hollywood forced their way into the region.

There were many Hollywood movies filmed in the region over the years at the Bradshaw Ranch and also a few filmed at the Hancock Ranch. There were more than a few tales circulating according to the Hancock's who lived close by that some of the Hollywood adventurers would get lost ending up visiting back in the day wearing strange costumes ranting strange tales.

Some of these encounters along with other strange events like seeing strange lights and large dark hairy animals had Mary Hancock and Bob Willard very alarmed at times who were way too eager to relate the experiences with the hair on their arms standing up of Skinwalker/Bigfoot creatures who were said to of even tormented people while inside "Secret Cabin" and later somehow tearing it apart. The cabin itself wasn't a secret but whatever was happening up at the place was known to all but the local tourists.

According to Bob Willard, there was a supernatural being who resided in the mountains even the local natives knew about stating:

"Native Americans believe there was a creature who lived in the area who tormented settlers who had somehow sinned against the people and land."

The description of the creature and the location has to make one wonder if this wasn't a place for the Mongolian Monster reportedly seen by many people over the years. The fact there were "Giant Skeletons" found close in the region as reported in the Prescott newspaper gives some substance to all the rumors. *Does this possibly also connect to why people have been reportedly gone missing in the region as presented in Verde Valley Bigfoot: The Missing 411?*

8 HIGHEST UFO ACTIVITY

In the Verde Valley, is Sedona, a small, tranquil city of 10,000 people that has become legendary in New Age circles for its enigmatic energies, vortexes, Native American legends of supernatural entities roaming the surrounding countryside, and much more of a paranormal/strange nature. Sedona is also home to the famous *Red Rocks Mountains*, large and stunning formations of sandstone that glow an eerie and captivating red and orange when the sun both rises and sets and which add even further to Sedona's reputation as a place of deep mystery and wonder.

According to the History Channel Sedona in recent years has had the highest UFO traffic in the northern hemisphere. Some claim the Angel Valley area has the highest per capita rate of UFO sights in the whole United States. Ex-State Senator *Dave Schmidt* stated on TV stating:

"There's more UFO sightings here in the greater Sedona area than anywhere else in the world."

It is also well known among fourteen researchers that Sedona host some of the most intense UFO, paranormal, metaphysical, and spiritual activity in the world causing fringe businesses to spring up. Many UFO sightings have been viewed near the major vortex areas out in nature leading to scenic adventures of the west.

Arizona is definitely more active than most states in the U.S. and the Sedona/Verde Valley is a major hotspot for UFO activity. The reasons remain a mystery, however, researching the region and from indigenous-American folklore, Arizona is considered by many to be an ethereal place, a spiritual vortex if you will. Under close examination anyone can begin to understand after some digging there is some basis to all the rumors.

Recorded UFO sightings in the region go back perhaps further than most realize. The surrounding countryside is full of ancient petroglyphs depicting flying suns or what some consider *"Orbs."* The people of the time must have been seeing something in order to take the time to draw the events in stone.

Image above: Honanki Heritage site next to the Bradshaw Ranch and Angel Valley Labyrinth is one of the largest cliff dwellings of the Red Rock country created between AD 1150 - 1350. The site is managed by the U.S. Forest Service for a reason. *(Public domain.)*

"Are these perhaps some of the oldest recorded UFO encounters in the region?"

Throughout the Sedona/Verde Valley region, the cliff walls speak volumes all making the mystery and clues stand out for anyone to interpret. Of course, it should be duly noted that it seems a little odd people are reportedly seeing, capturing excellent photos and videos, of what the ancient American Indians were drawing on the local cliff walls in stone 100's of years ago. This connection is a little hard to ignore.

"UFO Tours with Guaranteed Sightings"

Costing roughly $3,500 per pair, the goggles are pretty badass. They amplify 20,000 times more light than is capable of being seen by the naked human eye. Nightly tours go out with visitors equipped with night vision glasses, binoculars, and telescopes. According to many accounts, it's in the last hour of twilight when many of these phenomena take place and the amount of activity recorded is staggering! One person going on of the local tours to see a UFO reported:

"I went out on a UFO Tour with Anita Owens and was blown away by the UFO sightings that everyone had on this tour. Looking through her night-vision googles made viewing the ships on the ground in the canyon so clear! It was truly awesome! We all saw 3 large glowing balls of light merge into one ball of light and change color to a bright pink ball, so bright that it could be seen with the naked eye! What an extraordinary experience. A must-do when visiting Sedona! Thank you, Anita, for sharing your extensive knowledge of UFO and paranormal experiences."

Another person reported:

"My husband, Cody, and myself went out with Anita Owens Friday evening, this is our second trip to do the paranormal

experience. It was absolutely amazing. There was more activity during our recent outing than any of us could have expected. UFO'S landing, thrusting up and down, wormholes, flying rods, so many things came up in my pictures besides just UFO'S that it has made me a true believer that there is so much out there beyond just us."

Image above: 2013 *"A Flying Sun in Arizona at Sunset Point."* (It looks like the sun is setting at Sunset point when the real sun is still up in the sky above the clouds.) The ancients felt compelled for some mysterious reason to carve/paint drawings of flying suns on the local mountains in the form of petroglyph which are protected by the U.S. Forest Service at the Honanki Heritage site and others. *(Public domain.)*

To find local businesses in the Sedona/Verde Valley region that advertises they will ensure a person will see all kinds of UFO activity both in the sky and landing on the mountains around Sedona is mind-bending. Sedona UFO & Vortex Tours, boasts on their website, "I GUARANTEE SIGHTINGS!" A "UFO Sighting Guarantee" is just too good to pass up. UFO sighting tour falls outside the boundaries of a "normal" travel tour. However, this remarkable venture ran by Anita Owens has plenty of videos and eyewitness accounts to put the Sedona/Verde Valley region on top for having the most sightings.

To have UFO sightings in the region is very common, so common the majority are not even being reported anymore but are now part of a budding supernatural tour experience sold off in businesses. Nevertheless, after going on the UFO sighting tour most people report they will never look up at the sky in the same way again because the phenomena has been happening for a very long time.

"Instead of being labeled and called crazy, some people decided to become entrepreneurs of the unexplained. The business has never been better."

Truly people have been flocking to the Sedona/Verde Valley region of Arizona for a far less tranquil reason than the beauty of the surrounding red rock mountains. A local evangelist and author, David Herzog, writes, "In the early 1900s Sedona was a place where Christians from all over the United States gathered to hold large conferences and retreats as God's glory filled the city"—long before it was claimed by the New Age movement.

Today the area is world-famous for its paranormal phenomena above all. Sedona, Arizona is by far one of America's most popular destinations for spotting UFOs. Today in the region seeing them has become so commonplace people have stopped reporting them. The fact a person can find thriving local UFO touring businesses equipped with night vision glasses who all guarantee UFO sightings clearly say the area is sacred and beyond magical.

The amount of activity recorded in the region is staggering including reported sightings of; Aliens, Bigfoot, Orbs, and portals, all within the red rock mountain desert. When *Angelheart*, the General Manager of *Nulemurian Heart Center* at Angel Valley, and others at the Angel Valley Labyrinth specifically state they have been catching many magical things appearing in the skies over the area and that it's been happening for years, well there just maybe something to all the rumors.

9 THE MERKABAH CONNECTION

Due to all the strange phenomena consisting of UFO sightings, government property takeovers, and so on documented taking place right around the Angel Valley Labyrinth location, it doesn't seem very far-fetched then for someone to say one of these beings landed and communicated with someone. It was through such "extraterrestrial communication" the founder was told to create the Angel Valley Labyrinth out in the desert instructing him to model it after the *Chartres Labyrinth* having within the center the flower of life and so much more.

Throughout the ages, there have existed societies for the study and elucidation of the Mysteries, into which none but the initiated could gain admission into these schools of mysticism. The knowledge which they acquired had to be kept within those sacred enclosures therefore it wasn't to be trusted to just anyone.

Merkabah mysticism is a school of early Jewish mysticism centered on visions found in the Book of Ezekiel chapter 1, and other texts, relating to stories of ascents to heavenly palaces. The Merkabah literature was composed in the period 200–700 CE, although later references can be found in the Middle Ages. Merkava mysticism began to flourish in Palestine during the 1st century AD. Some Jewish Mysticism would appear to be as old as the Jewish religion itself remaining the exclusive property of the initiated ones, preserved chiefly in the Enoch literature.

The noun Merkabah/Merkavah "*thing to ride in*" is derived from the Masoretic text of 1:4–26, the word is not explicitly an object that is caused or produced by something else in Ezekiel 1. Some Jewish biblical commentaries emphasize the imagery of the Merkabah should not be taken literally; but rather are analogies for the various ways that God reveals himself to his people. However, there are also warnings against the practicing of this legendary experience so a person is left to wonder what is the truth when the path isn't always clear. Perhaps the ancient Mishnah laying down the rule may show the answer:

"The Ma'aseh Merkabah should not be taught to anyone except he be wise and able to deduce knowledge through wisdom ('gnosis') of his own."

Further glimpses of the mysteries of the Merkabah may be discerned in other rabbinical sayings: "The angel Sandalfon towers above the rest of the angels the length of a five hundred years' journey; his feet touch the earth while his head reaches the holy Hayyot. He stands behind the Throne-Chariot binding wreaths for his Master."

Corresponding directly with *Metatron's Cube* the Merkabah has been called the divine light vehicle used by ascended masters over the ages to connect with the higher realms. *"Mer"* means Light. *"Ka"* means Spirit. *"Ba"* means Body. *Mer-Ka-Ba* is the spirit body surrounded by counter-rotating fields of light, (wheels within wheels), spirals of energy as in the structure of human DNA capable according to some of transporting the spirit body from one dimension to another.

By virtue of our DNA, the Merkabah is able to spiral a person out of this reality and spiral/spin them back from that reality to another. (6 pairs of twin strands - 6 is Star of David, Flower of Life, and Merkabah.) DNA, the ancient cabalistic *"Tree of Life"* portrayed in the Biblical Torah is viewed as a live waveform configuration, able to be modified by certain spoken words or tones.

In esoteric teachings, the Merkabah is an interdimensional vehicle consisting of two interlocked tetrahedra of light with a common center with one tetrahedron pointing up and the other down. This point symmetric form is called a stella octangula or stellated octahedron which can also be obtained by extending the faces of a regular octahedron until they intersect again. This star tetrahedron is a *"three-dimensional Star of David."*

Merkabah is shaped like a three-dimensional, six-pointed star, also known as a stellar tetrahedron. The top half of this star, which resembles a pyramid, symbolizes mankind ascent to God, and the bottom half represents God as it reaches down to mankind.

In Merkava mystical literature the ascent of the soul is described in detail as a perilous journey through seven spheres, otherwise termed "heavenly dwellings" to the final goal; enabling a person, while still in the flesh, to ascend into the presence of the eternal in the innermost palace before a supreme divine being seated on a throne surrounded by awesome hosts who sing God's praise.

Image above: An Angel flies over Red Rock Crossing in Sedona. *The Angel Valley Labyrinth was constructed on angelic instruction based on an 800-year-old design having within the center the blueprint for ascension as well as to be a gateway for interdimensional travel. (Public domain.)*

The Merkabah-Riders

Those who practiced Merkava were sometimes called *"Explorers of the Supernatural World"* (Yorde Merkava). Merkabah it is said requires a rigor of internal development lasting for a lifetime or for many lifetimes. It is not something that can be achieved as a result of following simple steps like meditation, scrying, or trying to decipher dream experiences. The select morally fit Merkabah initiates (tzenu'im), are required to prepare themselves by fasting and to use certain magical formulas (called seals) to placate the angelic gatekeeper of each heavenly dwelling.

Continued ablutions, fasts, fervent invocations, incantations, and other means is said to bring on an ecstatic state for those who enter upon the "Vision of the Merkabah" called Yorede Merkabah. The mystics by training themselves to a life of untarnished holiness were able to enter a state of ecstasy, to temporarily ascend into the unseen, and, having done so seen and learned the deepest mysteries.

These were the students of the Merkabah who, as a result of some peculiar mental makeup, were capable of reaching the goal of mastering the physical and metaphysical laws of karma. Under a strange hallucination, those who imagine themselves entering the heavenly realms are called "Yorede Merkabah." In this chariot, they are supposed to behold the innermost secrets of all persons and things, otherwise impenetrable and invisible.

Merkabah Riders transform their physical body into the "light body." It is said the physical body has to low vibration/density. In order to transform their physical bodies into the Merkabah, they create an energy field of light around themselves in order to separate from the lower vibrations. Through practice and training when vibrations reach a high level the Merkabah is activated. When a person begins to vibrate the correct spoken words, these higher frequencies form a geometric pattern which begins to merge the higher levels of consciousness, for sound has form surrounding the light body serving as a vehicle to travel through time, dimensions and space.

The ancient texts specifically show often metamorphically that in order to transform the physical body into the light one needs to create an energy field of light around the person performing the operation in order to separate from the lower vibrations. Once liberated there are 7 subtle bodies to experience each of the existing 7 planes of existence. Merkabah is said to be the tool that allows a person to experience a multidimensional journey.

Every Merkabah's is in a creative matrix connected to the source allowing access to soul intention with the spark of source energy allowing for the creation of any reality chosen programmed through initiation, meditation, and intentions. Active programming is very task-specific, detailed, and proactive; if a person is worthy of having mastered themselves (energy) they are granted access.

The seeker of the mysterious desiring to ride upon the *Chariot of Fire* gains access to the *"Divine Dimensions"* by the use of formulae or passwords which have the virtue of compelling the angels to grant admission. To undertake the perilous (Ierkabah) ride one must be of complete knowledge of the processes at work for there are depths to equal the heights to which one can be cast.

The warrior-nature of the angels surrounding the "inner chamber" shall keep anyone unworthy at bay with flames darting forth from their eyes as they ride upon fiery horses armed with weapons of fire. In order to be allowed to pass these terrible beings, the Merkabah Rider must prove him/herself. There is a description of the seven heavenly halls in some texts, each of which is guarded by angels who through the use of formula may be invoked.

In order to be able to shift between the various levels of existence, it is said the rider must know what is going on at all times being in complete control unafraid and MUST be protected. *Merkabah is a type of interdimensional suit used for ascension.*

The Arrival

Whether or not these special bodies are what some are seeing flying around through the region at night has been the speculation of some for a while who have been on the outside looking in at some of the strange assurances resulting in lots of conspiracy theories of what may be happening.

Are these ascended masters in their light body seen flying around or Angels, ETs, or something else in the area?

Is there some kind of supernatural light body training taking place somewhere in Sedona or is the area being visited or both?

One thing is for sure there is and has been something supernatural going on and it seems a lot of people have known about it for some time. All the hype has led to people coming to the area from all over the world seeking out the experiences so many brags upon.

Sedona became the nucleus of the New Age movement in the 80s when some 5,000 believers flocked from all over the world for the *"Harmonic Convergence."* Due to Native American legends of spots where the earth's energy is supposedly concentrated some people claim to experience a range of sensations that encourage self-healing and spiritual awakening within, *"The Vortex."*

The event began as an interpretation of the Mayan calendar; tens of thousands of people gathered around spiritual centers for meditation to protect the earth from spinning away into space. An important part of the Harmonic Convergence observances was the idea of congregating at power centers on earth where the spiritual energy strong. While praying for a global awakening, many of those who came to Sedona developed a deep astral connection to the red rock formations of the mysterious vortexes present here.

For decades afterward, more people have continued to arrive, to heal and to be healed. The tourists it seems have been seeking something authentic wanting traditional forms of enlightenment that goes back centuries. *The Center for the New Age* advertises itself as "Your New Age Super

(Natural) Store" for vortex information, UFO tours, and so much more.

In 2003 there was a total of 5 reported UFO Orb (flying sun) sightings. Then the numbers started to rise fast just before the year 2012-2013 when there were over 865 reportedly seen in the United States alone in just one year. (2012 into 2013 according to the Mutual UFO Network MUFON reached the point of saturation.) By 2014 there were 410 reported cases, less than half sighted than the year before, indicating there was a steep decline making 2012 the year of arrival. The Mayan Calendar predicted something would happen in 2012 calling it the "shift of the ages" which according to the data and some researchers took place.

New Age thought was the year marked the start of a period during which Earth and its inhabitants would undergo a positive physical or spiritual transformation marking the beginning of a new era, while others suggested the date marked a catastrophe or possibly even the end of the world. Nevertheless, according to all the reported sightings, many of which were caught on camera, something extraordinary happened in the United States.

"There were thousands of UFO sightings in the Sedona/Verde Valley region during 2012-2013."

10 PROJECTIONS

Having lots of reported supernatural activity of *Angels/ETs/Shapeshifters* etc., or whatever you want to call the "visitors" land in the Sedona region in great numbers and or appear in their "light body" can at times be a little frightening for those who are not ready to experience these types of events. The fact is nobody really has shown the ability to control whatever the flying balls of light do in any manner they just do what they do. The strange apparitions show up whenever they want to manifest it seems, not when a person wants them to show up scaring people in the process shining like the sun.

If for whatever reason a person is unable to climb aboard a UFO and be taken into the heavens above like *Enoch* was in the great Macrocosm there are other alternatives listed in the sacred texts handed down for getting in touch with and accessing the otherworldly realms. The esoteric scriptures describe in specific detain intentional out-of-body experience (OBE) in an "astral body" that is separate from the physical body capable of traveling outside it throughout the universe. This practice allows a person to travel beyond the material world using the mind.

According to some ancient traditions the physical body has an invisible double, the spirit, ethereal body, or astral body. The concept of astral projection hinges on the belief that in addition to our physical bodies, humans also have an "astral body," which is sometimes referred to as an etheric body, subtle body, or light body.
"The idea that humans can leave their bodies during dream states is ancient."

The *APA Dictionary of Psychology* defines the state as a hypothesized level of existence accessible to the consciousness or spirit, which acts as a link between the physical and spirit or divine worlds. Often the state is induced through various hallucinogenic and hypnotic means (including self-hypnosis) or using drugs and other means. Most practitioners believe their experiences are really just as a person who takes LSD or peyote is convinced of interacting with angels/demons or god while in their altered state.

An astral projection is an intentional effort to send consciousness from the body to another location. It refers to consciousness traveling out of the body toward a spiritual plane or dimension. Leaving the body on command is often linked to lucid dreaming, or the ability to control your dreams.

Out-of-body experiences often hinge on the soul separating from the body, implying a distinction between the two that science and researchers do not yet support. However, the concept is explored in various religious texts in detail, including the ancient Hindi and Qur'an scriptures. Even ancient Egypt had a concept of the soul separate from the physical body. The astral plane is considered to be the home of not only souls finding their way onward to their next life or final resting place, but also angels/demons and spirits.

Some say that the astral body emerges from the physical body through the Third Eye or from the crown chakra believed to be one of the Siddhis achievable by yoga practitioners through self-discipline and practice. It has been pointed out that in the celebrated Indian epic *The Mahabharata*, Drona leaves his physical body to see if his son is alive.

In the 2016 blockbuster "*Doctor Strange*," a superhero is known as the "Master of the Mystic Arts" able to commune with cosmic intelligence through visions and vivid experienced during astral projection intentionally sending consciousness from his body to another location on command.

Frontiers of Human Neuroscience published an article in which researchers observed a subject's brain while she claimed to be in a state of astral projection with an MRI who was able to successfully identify unique parts of the brain that were active during her metaphysical journey. Having some evidence something is happening in one's head during such a journey may not be able to prove that your soul is out on an adventure in the cosmos, but it's an indication that there's some interesting brain activity happening within pointing to an altered state.

Legend says from the astral world we come at birth, and there we shall return at death. Suppose that in the dream state a person were to take a trip to Sedona to visit the Angel Valley Labyrinth and do some meditation in the center. From there according to legend a person can travel to visit the pyramids in Egypt before rounding out the night on another dimension.

Image above: Scrying mirror and crystal ball. Whether or not these devices work is matter of speculation to some. Nevertheless, the people who do use them believe they do work from which a market for the devices has existed for very a long time. (Some scrying mirrors use another example of a type of "mantra" along the boards to help focus attention.)

Taking the matter further are those who not only claim to be able to use the arcane abilities successfully but have in their possession tools created to specifically assist in accomplishing the task. Projecting themselves into these objects some claim the ability to travel into various otherworldly places. Scrying is a type of divination performed by gazing into a smooth often dark surface in order to receive messages, guidance, or visions from the spirit world with a tradition going all the way back to ancient Egypt.

Everyday devices we have in our pockets with smooth black screens can be used for scrying and are used for such purposes outright as it is with the information, they are able to provide. Of course, the use of some of these devices is forbidden in some ancient texts. Nevertheless, using a computer as a phone, or other similar devices are in fact modern versions of these ancient tools.

Matters of the soul have always been to date incredibly hard to study in a laboratory setting or explain. Some say astral projection is very much possible, while others say it's not. Almost all Astral projection information is anecdotal. Pinning down human consciousness within the realm of modern science has proven at times to be difficult. Whether a person chooses to believe in astral projection or not will ultimately come down to their own experiences of human consciousness.

Image above: "The Separation of the Spirit Body" from *The Secret of the Golden Flower*, a Chinese handbook on alchemy and meditation shows the process through which people are able to change form and travel to otherworldly places. "*Although there are two different people, their faces*

and clothes are exactly alike. Clearly, he is a divine immortal who can divide his body and appear in several places at once."

The Way of the Dreamer

Offering a glimpse of alternative worlds just as real as this one to the dreamer while dreaming, many glimpse the mystical worlds beyond the parameters of the rational mind of mundane reality naturally all the time each night when they go to sleep. Entering into this magic dimension is something we do all the time. Many of us of course are too busy chasing the dream in the real world to pay much attention to what lurks below the surface within ourselves. The world has created many distractions to lead one away from the source and center of consciousness itself. Yet with or without our conscious awareness the place of dreams still exists and herein is where many masters say the true work begins. To the masters, taking control of one's dreams is the true source of power. But what kind of power? Power is not controlling others, no it is found in controlling the self. Trying to control another human being is a sign a person is actually in most cases entirely out of control for controlling others is what weak people think power is and looks like. In order to understand the position of dreamer v. dreaming one has to comprehend the unwarranted influence to want to have control over others.

Only those who have passed through the gates of dreaming can relate the experience leading to true freedom. The one who has gained control of the self in dreaming is the person who has mastered the self-wherein is found an ancient launch pad within the labyrinth acting as a transported pad ultimately leading to the unseen realms of ancestor spiritual forces and beyond. Like the layers of an onion, according to some experts, there are worlds within our own which can be visited through dreams described as a type of "gateway to infinity." The existence of these mystical places are independent and constant despite our awareness of them for the soul-the true self-never sleeps always moving about in the spiritual worlds. As windows into worlds beyond the ordinary dreams touch every level of our lives.

Many religious books speak of dreams/visions and how they are used by spiritual forces to guide people along the way in the human experience throughout the ages. Gaining insight into the psychology of dreaming is something that has been taking place for a very long time. For some, like the elite, dreams which are not interpreted are like emails which are never opened.

For a lot of the untrained interpreting dreams is often difficult because people are not used to the symbolic language used by the ancients to communicate with the dreamer that he/she is the dream. It is by focused concentrated attention that we as humans are able to establish contact with the otherworldly and thereby are able to communicate. The spiritual adventures that can be attained through dreams gives a person's soul wings indeed, however, there is a few tricks a person must learn first before they are able to safely fly. In the dream world a person can make themselves miserable, or happy, just as in this world. Of course, many are still lost in is life really a dream and if so who's the dreamer: what's the dream?

"Discover who you truly are, otherwise, you will have to depend on other people's opinions who don't even know themselves. Other people are not the way nor are they medicine."

For centuries the act of entering dreams has been described as the gateway into the inner self. gaining a better understanding of our dreams is no easy task for they are connected to our unconscious and subconscious. The unconscious is the realm of the shadow wherein is a dense maze of all one hopes to be and the monsters of a thousand lifetimes. Using the magical tool of the labyrinth to lead one through twists and turns deeper within the self carries one into the magical realm which often leads to discoveries and questions. What really is a labyrinth? What are their meaning and message?

Although labyrinths seem to be a tool of mystery to most people the fact is the first constructed were anchored to the earth. From the huge stone labyrinth found at the base of Mount Hermon to the Angel Valley Labyrinth in Sedona, Arizona, a person will find a connection to the earth itself. Each time a person walks the path of the labyrinth they are grounding themselves. The entrance is the portal inside for integration and magical working in order to be able to walk between worlds for the labyrinth not only floats on the earth plane existing as a doorway but also goes much further into the "As above, so below."

When it comes to achieving dream control by becoming aware of and commanding in another world one begins to realize the dream is indeed alive pulsating with the brilliance of energy. Everything a person perceives is energy, but for some reason, we are not experiencing everything as energy, but are more to fit things into a classification mold as an object separate from the whole. Instead of seeing energy directly from the source we see identification which tends to separate. For the dreamer, the most significant act of dreaming is to see the universe as it really is acknowledging its spellbinding powers for what they are.

Over the years many have developed techniques for taking control of the personality through various means like fasting, sustaining from drugs, sex, etc., basically performing curtain rites in order to facilitate a specific result in order to put a leash on their animal nature and train it. Devising such extravagant techniques have produced results of altered states of consciousness and other benefits like dream control. Of course, some of these ancient practices are naturally beneficial which is why they are sometimes found within churches like fasting. When the human body becomes hungry it begins to eat itself in a cleansing process removing sick cells like cancer. When the body is ready it gathers around the dead cells and dissolves them restoring the body.

THE SEVEN GATES

For most the seven wonders of the world are being able to feel, to hear, to laugh, to love, to see, to taste, and to touch. These places show there are doorways through which some kind of conscious awareness/interaction is taking place. The rabbit hole goes somewhat deeper when it comes to the "Seven Gates" of dreams/dreaming. According to some forms of shamanism, as well as gnostic texts, and others, there are seven gates of dreaming.

Everyone on earth is at the first gate with being in the physical universe. Corresponding with the body within the each person reaches the threshold of the first gate when they become aware they are falling asleep suspended in the heaviness of darkness. To be able to consciously pass through the gate attention must be focused so precise it must get down to the size of a cell or 100th the width of a hair. It is no easy process.

There are some short cuts of course learned by the masters like that of passing through the hourglass on the Black Widow spider among other supernatural/natural techniques which won't be gone into any detail here. For us tot76 perceive these other realms a person has not only to become aware of them but also has to covet them as well with sufficient energy to be able to seize their existence. It is at the first gate one learns to become aware they are falling asleep and that dreams are, if not a hatch, but doorway into other worlds. Of course, dreams can be a two-way passage place as well for in the other realms are scouts who tend to want to enter into our world which is why for some, they use rituals of protection.

The Second Gate is found in the realm of lucid dreaming. Dreaming attention is the key to just about every movement in the dream world. The Third Gate is Astral Projection having what some call out of body experience (OBE's). The Fourth Gate leads to shared dreams with the dreaming with others. The rest will be explained in more detail in the next update.

11 THE HARMONIC CONVERGENCE

There are lots of people in the Sedona/Verde Valley region who have seen a lot of strange glowing phenomena up in the sky in the last couple of decades. Some local residents have surmised maybe a few of the spiritual gurus in the area are actually doing their job causing their students to truly ascend becoming so enlightened they are rumored to be seen flying around in their light body leaving this world on adventures. These legends/myths wouldn't normally be taken seriously by most but the area has reportedly an extremely high rate of strange phenomena including disappearances to go along with all the evanescent sightings.

In the book *"Legends of the Verde Valley,"* it was reported there was a rumor the area has the highest rate of people vanishing in the state per capita. Of course, normally this type of statement wouldn't be very alarming, however, to of discovered through research Arizona ranks up top in the nation with Alaska for the strange permanent abductions to who can say where is rather alarming.

Prior to the *Harmonic Convergence* in the 80s the Sedona/Verde Valley region had actually been a predominately Christian landscape where people would come on retreats to study the bible with their family. The Harmonic Convergence world's first synchronized global peace meditation held on August 16th and 17th in 1987 described as a "grand conjunction" seemed to consist of the perfect alignment of people and planets. People wanted to be in Sedona with the rest of the so-called spiritual masters for alignment to be a part of the broadcasted grand event by the mystics. They came from all over the world to be a part of something larger than themselves. Afterward, some never left have stayed in the region becoming part of the mystic community.

Image above: Newspaper article of the two day "planetary Woodstock" of Sedona, Arizona in 1987.

Said to be the "Zero Point" when the Earth's maximum energy and magnetic fields would prepare our "manifest physical bodies" for "The Shift of the Ages" of complete repatterning of the expression of human consciousness the event become a media circus attracting all kinds of strange people. Organizers and participants called it everything from 'a planetary Woodstock' to 'the dawn of a new age,' while skeptics dismiss it as summer madness in the desert heat.

CBS News reported, "If we play our cards and our flutes and our wind chimes right, we could be in for a New Age of peace and love." At the time, it seems some people must have been unhappy with the state of the world. "*We have to do something*," said one woman. "*We have a responsibility to change the consciousness on the planet.*"

Then for whatever reason, before and afterward, there soon came an influx of all types of people into the area some claiming to be spiritually minded looking to help others or others to receive instruction. Soon the vortex phenomena took off among others. From there the area really started to flourish in the supernatural arena with all kinds of occultists like *Anton Levey, Israel Regardie,* and a host of others who were drawn to the region with others of their kind. Within 5 years Linda Bradshaw started to see her first flying light balls cruising through the sky along with her husband Bob inspiring her to write the book, "*Merging Dimensions.*"

Anyone who has ever taken a close look at the New Age Movement can attest to it being a very complex religious philosophy of many sources. It's best known as the movement that spread through the occult and metaphysical religious communities in the 1970s and '80s. With the Vatican at the *Sedona Chapel of the Holy Cross,* famous occult residents like *Antone Lavey* and *Isreal Regardie,* (the personal aid to Alester Crowley) plus over 4+ million visitors a year, there's really no question about it, "Sedona is the New Age Capital of the World."

As the reigning champion of the movement, Sedona soon became a place where the Shaman, Magicians, Wizards, Witches, etc., came together to not only be together but more importantly be able to openly show their powers and ultimate worth to the growing collective.

"If a person can believe in crystals, horoscopes, and ghosts, why can't they believe in themselves? In essence, the person is having more faith in an object like a rock than their own minds."

Finally, after all the evidence to date, it must be asked:
"*Why are all the top famous occultists and even the Vatican itself (Chapel of the Holy Cross) drawn to the Sedona/Verde Valley area?"Were they drawn to Sedona's fledgling New Age Movement to assist in its development to become the New Age Capital of the World or were they compelled for other reasons? What is it about the Sedona/Verde Valley area that attracts so many people from all walks of life?*

Looking back, it seems something really wanted the Bradshaw's attention enough to scare them in order to attempt to force them off their valuable land. The Bradshaw's and neighbors Hancock's were cattle ranchers who valued privacy and loved the red rock mountain landscape. Before the end, and before, each knew the worth of their land and neither wanted to sell it.

Sedona become known as "*little Hollywood*" after there had been so many western movies filmed in the region. Before the occult came into town and Hollywood filming its many movies specifically Westerns at the Bradshaw Ranch nobody ever complained about anything supernatural or strange. Of course, there was an occasional UFO sight, and Native American folklore stories about *Montezuma Well*, but nothing like what soon came after Hollywood and the occult showed up, nor after the Harmonic Convergence. Then all of a sudden, it seemed out of nowhere in the early 90s onward into 2012 the region was said to of becoming a type of galactic airport where portals opened up and aspirations were seen coming through terrorizing Sedona residents according to some witnesses.

Some locals surmised the influx of the occult, famous for summonsing entities and opening portals, was the cause for the growing unexplained phenomena, while others thought the tales were made up myths to simply scare people off the land. However, it wasn't long before TV shows were sending out film crews to investigate all the rumors, who for themselves, were not only seeing the phenomena but were also capturing on camera the events as well.

No doubt it became clear something supernatural was taking place in the Sedona/Verde Valley getting national attention enough to attract the U.S. Government who decided they needed/wanted to acquire the land by forming and using *The Land Preservation Task Force*. Although some years later some have claimed bits of the land have been sold off to the top bidders. USA Today called Sedona the most beautiful place in America not long afterward. "Some have surmised it was Hollywood and the occult who opened up the portals to chase people off their supernatural valuable land."

12 SHAMANIC JOURNEYS: OPEN THE GATE

Whether it was all the UFO traffic, Harmonic Convergence, Hollywood films, or all news coverage of strange phenomena, nobody can say for sure, but something started to attract an assortment of people into the Sedona/Verde Valley who began to appear selling their way of life. It wasn't long before self-help to paranormal books thrived giving rise to psychic palm/tarot card readings, UFO/ghost tours, and other assortments of paranormal/spiritual guidance activities/centers which seemed to of sprang to life overnight. Sedona soon became known as the *"New Age Capital of the World."*

Some of the native Americans residing in the area jumped on board with the vortex phenomena who began to give mystic tours as well as opening up their sweat lodges to the public for vision quests and other mystical ceremonies. Not very many people from other countries or the U.S. for that matter had been inside a real sweat lodge before so going to experience one while on vacation was an attraction for many. Some performed the service for free, or for donations, while others viewed the sacred ceremony to be something worth exploiting for personal gain.

On October 8, 2009, at a "Spiritual Warrior" retreat conceived by New Age guru *James Author Ray* at the *Angel*

Valley Retreat Center took up to 60 attendees (sweat lodges usually consist of no more than 20 people) who paid up to $10,000 to participate in a vision quest exercise in a makeshift sweat lodge to experience what he called a "catalyst for personal transformation." The program promised several days of introspection, lectures, and cleansing exercises.

With more than 60 people crammed into a space of 415 sq ft, hot rocks were added into the fire pit, then doused with water to create steam which ultimately turned the enclosure into a human cooking pot. "You are not going to die. You might think you are, but you are not going to die," Ray said, according to attendees.

Emergency responders arrived at what one first took for mass suicide, according to a witness. People were dead and many others were suffering. After a four-month trial, James Arthur Ray was found guilty of negligent homicide and sentenced to prison.

In the aftermath investigators found Ray misrepresented himself and his organization as a true sweat lodge ceremony and facilitator. For one thing, in real sweat lodges, women are not allowed, yet Ray thought it was perfectly alright. Native American experts criticized Ray's construction of the structure as well as his ignorance of actually how to properly perform the ceremonies. The Native Americans stated Ray had no connection to any Native American community nor training in how to lead an actual sweat lodge citing permission to lead lodges is only granted to those raised in the ceremonial ways, and after many years of apprenticeship with Elders.

In 2020, an investigative journalist produced the true-crime podcast "Guru: The Dark Side of Enlightenment" after people started to complain Ray went back to the same ways after getting out of prison selling spiritual enlightenment for profit.

Image above: Investigators try to piece together why people ended up dead in a poorly made makeshift sweat lodge next to the Angel Valley Labyrinth outside Sedona, Arizona. (Public domain)

The Angel Valley Retreat Center was without question a booming business at one time until Ray showed up. People came from all over the world to experience the wonders of personal transformation and experience otherworldly events. It appears someone saw the special gathering and saw the potential to manipulate the good spiritual intent for personal gain. Angel Valley ended up taking Ray to court for all the loss in revenue as a result of the incident. Can't say we blame them. Perhaps the Native Americans should next.

Opening the Gates

When it came to exposing the secrets of the sweat lodge it seems James Author Ray didn't have a clue. In 1873 Native American religious rituals were banned by the U.S. government which included all sweat lodges. Many of the rituals were lost over time (generations) and have been kept a closely guarded secret not given to anyone outside the tribe. Non-indigenous persons are not normally given access to this information but somehow Ray considered himself an expert on American Indian traditions selling the so-called spiritual experience to those seeking fulfillment in those types of experiences without knowing what they were getting into. No doubt everyone involved experienced more than they could have imagined.

People at the time didn't question James Author Ray's ability to put them in touch with the spirit realm. It seems each was looking for something beyond the norm and was willing to pay a hefty price to experience the mystical state of being a spiritual warrior.

Most American Indian traditions of medicine wheels, sacred circles, vortexes, and the ability to open portals to enter into otherworldly places are very similar to some occult practices of placing the self-inside the "sacred circle" in order to make contact. Making contact is the goal between worlds or dimensions where entities, beings, gods, etc., are said to reside. It is the doorway through which the shaman begins his or her ecstatic quest from the physical to the spiritual plane. In a ritualistic trance the shaman's "breath-body" searches the interstices of the spirit world for a specific cure or a personal vision to bring back to the tribe.

The technology used for accessing and going into these mythical levels of consciousness shows the Native Americans use a number of ancient yet advanced technologies to enter these otherworldly places. In the sweat lodge, the drumming has a way of integrating and connecting with nature like the beating of one's own heart, the fire, steam, and other aspects are assigned roles for peeking experience along the path.

These transpersonal states of consciousness of spiritual and energetic makeup can be accessed making a proper shaman like a lighthouse using the language of sound/light geometry. It is a bridge, a teaching unto itself. The process is coded with information. By taking the non-ending journey within and the non-ending journey without, people are able to more effectively link up to the universal truth of all existence.

Each person enters the cavity in a clockwise motion seeking to become enlightened or to connect with the source. After being warmed in the fire and baptized in the steam, the practitioner travels upon the whims of the Shaman's voice who takes the person on a vision quest. Afterward, each person emerges from the "womb" soaking wet born anew taking the first breath of fresh air.

The world's greatest spiritual teachers from ancient to modern times have all basically shared the specific perception that the deepest truth of our being is not the property of one particular religion or spiritual tradition, but is found within the center of each person.

Perhaps it would be the end of all religions is realizing God in the individual soul. However, to be perfectly fair, a person could show someone a soul, even their own, and the person would most likely perceive it not.

13 SCHUMANN RESONATOR LABYRINTH

The Chartres Cathedral was built in 1220. Then 800 years later in 2020 the world was given *Schumann Resonators* which electrical boxes when plugged into the wall produce electromagnetic radiation tuned to 7.83 Hz which is the same frequency that the earth/atmosphere system "rings" at when the Earth is struck by lightning. The frequencies, created from thunderstorms and lightning, range from 7.83 Hz, sometimes referred to the Earth's "heartbeat," to 33.8 Hz. *7.83 Hz is also a common frequency the human brain operates at.* The human brain, and more specifically our thoughts, are constantly firing off electric signals through electric pulses.

According to science everything is made up of energy. Our physical bodies have an energetic vibration and so do our thoughts and soul which you will experience in the next chapter. The Earth itself is made up of vast amounts of energy of an electromagnetic grid which is and can be measurable; this is called *The Schumann Resonance.* In 1952 physicist *Winfried Otto Schumann* developed a mathematical equation to measure the Earth's magnetic frequency.

If a person is found to be out of sync with *Earth's Frequency* (Schumann Resonance) and not grounded one will begin to exhibit signs of discomfort that can range from anxiety, insomnia, illness, suppressed immune and so on.

Some have discovered that when humans are in sync with 7.83hz the body is somehow able to heal and increase its vitality. When some people have been exposed to the Earth's natural frequency of 7.83 Hz, they reportedly experienced such benefits as *"enhanced learning/memory, body rejuvenation, improved stress tolerance,"* and other benefits. It seems the ancients knew about this as well. As a global society it seems collectively, we have lost touch with our inner being or soul.

The *Chartres Labyrinth* next to a *Schumann Resonator.*

The connections between the Chartres Labyrinth and the Schumann Resonator are indeed remarkable under close examination. The electrical grid creates and harmonizes a frequency closely related to alpha waves (8-12 Hz). Occurring when a person is in a relaxed state without concentrating, like what is found in meditation, alpha waves fall in the middle of the brain wave spectrum. Alpha brainwaves are some of the most easily observed and were the first to be discovered. Alpha brain waves can occur while awake or in the initial phase of sleep.

Brainwaves occur at various frequencies, some being fast and some slow. Increasing alpha waves can stimulate creativity lowering depression and other symptoms. Using electricity to communicate with each other billions of neurons fire in a network linked to specific states of consciousness.

Meditation and mindfulness techniques to some may seem like mind control but the truth is more subtle. Besides feeling relaxed, alpha waves are in a way responsible for changing our mood. The next time you get stressed or depressed, one may think about what and how the brain is doing what it is and help it calm down or get energized using mind over matter techniques. Understanding the activity of the brain can help with sleep, stress, focus, and so much more.

If you're interested in any form of mental or physical self-mastery, you'll want to know about hacking into brain waves and what they have to teach us for the possibilities are endless. Brain science is indeed complex, but interesting and well worth investigating. For someone who is involved in personal wellness and self-mastery, it's probably the most interesting to learn to activate at will.

Walking the labyrinth is a purposeful walking meditation into not only the journey to reach the center where one encounters the silence and mystery of the inner soul. Anyone who takes a walk into the Angel Valley labyrinth or others like it do indeed experience a peace in the center where its like time and the world stands still for a moment. The energy found at labyrinths have been felt by many the reason they have become so popular.

A Schumann Resonator Labyrinth Coil says there may be something to these mysterious structures after all. If you've always thought they are in churches were just for decorating, maybe it's time to revisit your position. Electricity is not a modern thing as we were taught at school. Our history and potential have always been hidden.

14 SOUL JOURNEY: LAYING ON OF HANDS

The only reason James Author Ray and so many others like him are able to mislead people is that they have lacked a true knowledge of self which is often difficult for some to find due to the demands of everyday life where so many lose themselves. The world is indeed a very cruel and nasty place at times causing people to become unsatisfied. During such times the path leads many to seek otherness in the spiritual or perhaps redemption which can only be found from within and is wrought out by the soul itself with much endeavor and strain of the spirit.

Science has claimed it has mapped the brain and mind through experimentation yet what do we as a species really know about the soul? *Where does it come from and what is it?* Every person being a unique autonomous center of energy, an individual consciousness, a soul, will, is an inward star shining and existing by its own inward light which is very experiential as you are about to see.

"The Eyes are the window to your soul." - William Shakespeare

Without question, thousands of years ago ancient cultures knew about the Pineal Gland and its importance. Today, it appears there are forces determined to keep people in the dark about the portal that lies deep within the central part of our brains. The supernatural gateway is considered by many including governments to be a portal that connects the physical and spiritual world a way of traveling between dimensions, referred by many as astral projection or remote viewing. It appears modern medicine knows little about the gland's role, however, there is a rich metaphysical history. For example, Descartes believed the pineal was the 'seat of the soul' and both Western and Eastern mystical traditions place our highest spiritual center within its confines."

Throughout our lives we have been perhaps looking in the wrong place for self-realization. Truly for some the path is within it seems while others are attracted to an ever-changing outer world. Yet clues remain nevertheless of the doorways to otherworldly places.

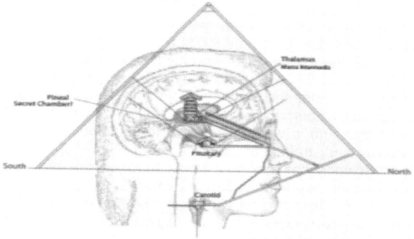

Image above: The Holy of Hollies is found within the innermost chamber... The eye of Horus (in the brain) aka the thalamus (meaning inner chamber) and the pyramid head superimposed with the King's inner chamber. (Public domain)

The inner chamber (Holy of Hollies found within the innermost chamber) is called the "vaulted chamber, the archway" where the flame (light) of the mind burns, where the torch bears the solitary candle "at the center of it all, your eyes." In Freemasonry, this is also the location of the "eternal flame." JRR Tolkien called it "the flame imperishable" (This is an alternate name of the Holy Spirit in Tolkien's mythos) or "The Secret Fire."

"The eye is the window to the soul." - Proverbs 30:17

At the center of it all is the light of consciousness found in places like the Olympic Torch/Freemasonry symbolizing keeping the sacred fire (spirit) burning at the seat of the soul. This same torch is said to be able to bear light through the underworld and is also the spiritual "all-seeing" eye, the eye you see with while dreaming.

"Enlighten means awaken to what we do and what's true, with eyes closed, there comes light in the mind. Enlightenment means light in the mind."

This torch is said to be surrounded by a *"Holy Guardian Angel."* These clues left behind by others have over the ages led to discoveries about the true nature of our being which under close examination is fundamentally awe-inspiring.

The Pineal Gland is one of the most enigmatic parts of the human body. The notion of a secret doorway in the head is something rather difficult to explain, yet the presence of this natural wonder within each person is undeniable for it is indeed experiential.

Shaped very similar to that of a pine cone this mysterious is located near the center of the brain and is also referred to as the "third eye." The pineal was—and is—something of an enigma still. Rene Descartes held it as the seat of the soul. Scientists have referred to the pineal gland as the atrophied third eye. Indeed, it, along with the pituitary, is the third eye chakra or energy center. Jesus said, *"The kingdom of heaven is within."*

After decades of relying on external sources of authority, it's surprisingly difficult for many to feel comfortable placing trust and confidence in themselves. You have been and had the "Holy Ghost" all along.

Image above: Pineal Gland is a small endocrine gland in the center of our brain that regulates: mood, immune system, circadian rhythms, aging, and so on. It releases an electrical portion - DMT/golden melatonin/honey. It is connected to the Pingala nerve. More blood flows per cubic volume to this special area than any other organ. The pineal gland is surrounded and bathed in cerebrospinal fluid. (Public domain)

According to some in the distant past, a man was in touch with the inner worlds through an activated pineal and pituitary gland called "The Eye of God" which was normally passed down by the laying on of hands from a master. Not too many people have truly discovered the true potential of this part of our body, however, many experts suggest that this gland is even more powerful and complex than the brain. The human eye in itself contains its very own universe, its own galaxies, for whatever is seen from the eye comes from the eye of the whole universe itself. Trusting the universe within one realizes the eyes are your truth leading on a path of discovery.

For many, the third eye is a personal gift to connect to the source and remind all of a universe much more mystical than that which is perceived with our physical senses. It's through the awakening of the pineal gland according to legend people attain supernatural feats of telepathy, psychic vision, etc., and have an intimate connection with God. Once a revered tool of seers and mystics, it's now for the most part become largely dormant, its divine purpose lost to most, however, its significance appears in every culture throughout the world.

The physical eyes perceive only a physical world, the third eye sees the true world—a unified whole with an unyielding connection to God. In this way, it has been said the third eye acts as the captain's seat of our soul. Almost every esoteric tradition has heralded the third eye as a connection to spirit, the space between humans and God experienced in the human condition.

The 3rd eye is the most heavily targeted & poisoned gland in the human body mainly because of the spiritual influences this "pine cone" shaped gateway has on human awareness. A pineal gland closed off means the mind can be easily manipulated and deceived unable to look beyond what is presented before it. On the other hand, an open third eye acts much like a truth detector picking up on the subtle subliminal inconsistencies of lies often used as a veil to conceal someone's true intentions.

Apparently, this gland only starts to be functional once our "mind" remains unconscious and is the key that gives us access to other dimensions that are in fact our own dreams making this a portal between different realities. Just as Christ led the way by showing humanity the potential in humans it is up to each individual to find/activate/cultivate those godly powers within. By believing in yourself a person ultimately discovers and becomes "the magician within" capable of anything far beyond the boundaries of this reality. "There is light within a man of light, and he lights up the whole world. If he does not shine, he is darkness."

The interior of the pineal gland has retinal tissue composed of photoreceptor cells and is filled with vitreous fluid just like the eyes which are also remarkably wired to the visual cortex.

"Information is light; light is information. The more you become informed, the more you alter your frequency. We are electromagnetic light beings."

Humans are said to be able to only see 1% of the visible light spectrum meaning one can only see 1% of what is going on around us. In other words, people are unable to see the vast 99% of the world. In essence, the majority of existence is unseen. The eyes only see a small portion, however, according to legend, there is another eye that is said to be able to pick up the "higher frequencies" of the pineal gland.

This remarkable gateway is considered by many to be the *"Epicenter of Enlightenment"* — for its symbol has been found throughout history in cultures around the world symbolized as a Pinecone. The Center of spiritual practices throughout history was based around the activation of the Third Eye. Achieving this activation is considered to be the Great Awakening/Work of divine alignment of the Chakras ultimately pointing the way to the next level of human transcendence.

Image above: The legendary third eye also known as the seat of the soul housing what the ancients called the Divine Spark. "The light of the body is the eye: if therefore thine eye be single, thy whole body shall be full of light" This is why you see some Hindu women wearing a red dot on their foreheads in recognition and awareness of the star within. (Public domain)

It seems the ancients were trying to tell us something about the marvelous intricate workings of ourselves. Who could have ever thought the path was within or the seat of "The God-Within?" The body really is a temple, it's not supposed to be a graveyard.

People come from all over the world to the Sedona/Verde Valley seeking spiritual enlightenment from the so-called self-proclaimed spiritual masters without realizing they themselves are the gateway they seek to enter having for themselves "*The Divine Spark.*"

The human body is composed of billions of atoms. These atoms, through attraction, form countless specialized combinations. These combinations result in the differentiation that we see in the human body. Sense organs, bones, muscles, etc. All of these billions of atoms are composed of matter.

In the majority of human beings, this Divine Spark is asleep. Not only is it asleep, but it is also more than likely buried under a ton of low-vibrational muck. For the most part, mankind is completely unaware of the treasure all carry within. *"My people perish from lack of knowledge."*

If one can discover and rouse this spark to life nurturing its ember into a burning flame, it will eventually light up the surrounding darkness making a connection with the Divine Universe ultimately becoming a ticket out of the hell of density. If one can activate this connection and sincerely build upon it, one's freedom from the Wheel of Death-And-Rebirth is virtually assured as they are safely tucked underwings.

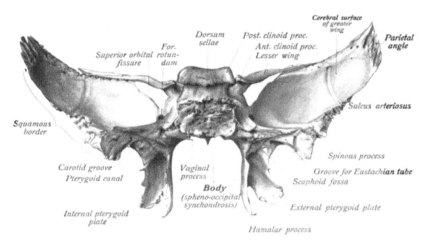

Image above: The sphenoid bone. The pituitary gland hangs just behind the Dorsum sellae in the Sella turcica surrounding the soul which some call the hidden yet literal "Angel within" having the visible wings thereof. (Public domain)

"The final mystery is oneself. When one has weighed the sun in the balance, and measured the steps of the moon, and mapped out the seven heavens star by star, there still remains oneself." — Oscar Wilde

The Laying on of Hands

In order to undertake this virtual "self-initiation ritual" of actually showing a person how to experience the light of their own "inner star" allowing for a small glimpse of the reflections within the soul, there must be some discussion. Indeed, being able to actually see and experience the "light" and the "soul" through the darkness may sound strange at first but as you are about to see it's very experiential.

There are two ways this practice can be done. It may be accomplished by the laying on of hands of one familiar with how to properly perform it as it should be done or by the self through a process of trial and error. As with all things, it's often better to have someone assisting who has traveled down the path and mastered the practice in order to get the desired results the quickest. Having an experienced facilitator is the best.

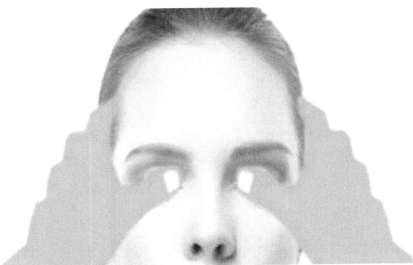

Image above: "The eyes truly are the gateway to the soul." A gateway to the soul truly can be found by peering through the eyes for through them the soul perceives. That doorway is also where the soul can actually be found and experienced by the "Laying on of Hands." (Public domain)

Through this gateway and the practices thereof, one is able to instantly journey to an inner place and start to have their eye become single and opened to the star and light within. The directions MUST be followed closely for there are dangers if this is practiced wrong like temporary blindness. Therefore, you will want to be in a safe and secure area since you will be vulnerable for a short period of time.

In essence, when in a dark place for a brief period of time, the eyes when firmly pushed on with the eyelids closed (thus the laying on of hands) by thumbs stops forward sight allowing the energy and power of sight to then be used to see by becoming redirected back to what is seeing. Using the power of the eyes sight is redirected back to the source. The eyes are a powerful gateway to our body, soul, and spirit. This experiential "Inner Light" actually comes from the soul which is already inside us protected by the wings of an angel guarding the ark within. The moment people are able to have knowledge of and free access to the soul, the more will see that this light is coming from somewhere they long to be.

Press and hold long enough (about 5 seconds) and the hidden realm of light will start to materialize forming kaleidoscopic geometric shapes and patterns similar to a honeycomb of light. The longer you can hold the gentle steady pressure and hold the eyes still, for the practice is rather uncomfortable, the more you will see.

Most people are not comfortable with the amount of pressure needed to produce the desired result. You literally have to exclusively trust the person performing the task as well because you are allowing them to put hands on you with eyes closed. Now of course you may see some light, but the light is not the result of your eyesight. Just about anyone can literally see light in the darkness, through the third eye thanks to neural pathways connecting the pineal gland to the visual cortex of the brain.

"The interior of our skulls contains a portal to infinity." ~ *Grant Morrison*

A gateway to gaze upon wherein a person is able to see a reflection of the soul which truly can be found by peering through the eyes for through them the soul itself perceives. "The eyes truly are the gateway to the soul."

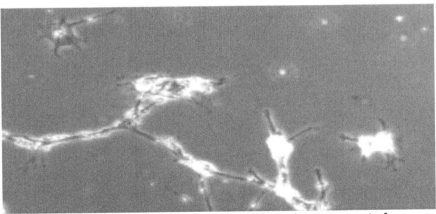

Image above: The human brain contains within a huge amount of energy stemming from source. When brain cells are placed into a culture dish together, they communicate and form connections.

If one follows the path correctly, after extensive research they will experience parts of themselves unaware of before and may peer into the dark abyss where there is no light but a single tiny cell. Through the electrical conduit of the eyes, this sense is able to see into the brain. It is from here the soul perceives and commands.

"The kingdom of heaven is inside of you; whosoever shall know himself, shall find it." -Egyptian Proverb

When done correctly a person begins to see the whole inside light up with the honey comb "flower of life" as well other grand design visionary images naturally flowing burning alive in the fire of the eyes. The exercise clearly shows that within each person is a light shining bright like the sun. It is said humans emit wavelengths of light undetectable to the naked eye. These ultraweak photon emissions in essence make us light beings who get our energy from the sun. The body is only able to access the frequencies of light by absorbing minerals which act as conduits for electrical activity.

In reality, humans are bioluminescent who actually glow visible light. However, the light emitted is around 1000 times lower in spectrum than the sensitivity of our naked eyes can see therefore we are not able to see this truth.

"Incredible amounts of energy are hidden in your brain; enough in a gram of flesh to run the city of Chicago for 2 days." Paramahansa Yogananda

Piezoelectric microcrystals inside the pineal gland according to scientists are said to be a link to higher dimensions acting like some type of cosmic antenna. There is a strong possibility that the complex twinned structure of the crystals may lower their symmetry and permit the existence of a piezoelectric effect. Interesting to note is the cubic, hexagonal and cylindrical morphologies identified using the electron microscope. Calcite ($CaCO_3$) is a hexagonal lattice system crystal that demonstrates the piezoelectric effect.

When calcite crystals are subjected to mechanical stress, they can generate an electrical charge or release light. There have been some suggestions calcite crystals in the pineal gland may turn it into a type of receiver that tunes in to different frequencies similar to a radio receiver (crystal radios use mineral crystals) perhaps being the connection where the pineal gland receives messages from spirit.

The pineal gland is a sensor of energy fields and can be influenced by electromagnetic radiation. Activating is said to allow clearer communication with higher realms allowing a person to achieve meaningful dreams and a deeper connection with spirit.

It therefore may not be a coincidence that calcite often occurs naturally. Amethyst is another piezoelectric crystal (it's a quartz variant) known to stimulate better sleep and dreams in order to assist a person to connect with mystical experience in higher realms. To some, the truth of reality is it has been funneled down into being mind/spirit, the literal stuff of dreams. On these terms, reality is the pure divine mind of the creator, a dream within the matrix.

Image above: Featured art: 'The Seer' (2018) by Alex Grey. Is there no wonder then why the band Tool, the front runner to the band Puscifer, who resides in the Sedona/Verde Valley region, used this guy's artwork for their album covers? (Public domain.)

It has been the writer's mission to make a soul perceivable to itself using a visionary journey of words forming and leading to visual imagery with a virtual laying on of hands in order to encourage the development and acknowledgment of inner sight and the self. To find the visionary realms one must enter through and use the intuitive inner eye of the soul, the eternal part where god meets God. It is at this point one realizes the most high does not dwell in temples made by human hands.

"Our greatest treasure is that which is hidden deep within our own subconscious, is that dark unused part of our self that is in fact light that is unconscious of itself." — Carl Jung

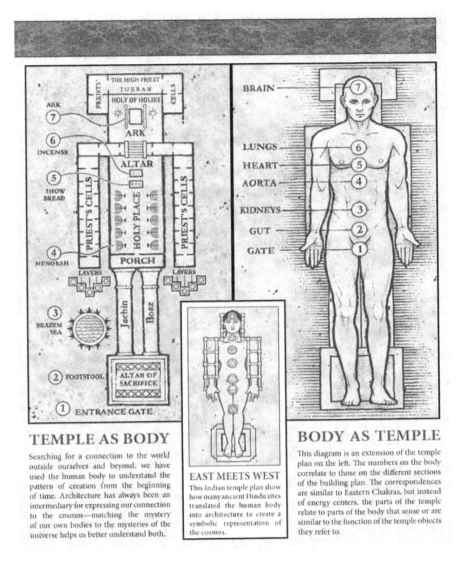

TEMPLE AS BODY

Searching for a connection to the world outside ourselves and beyond, we have used the human body to understand the pattern of creation from the beginning of time. Architecture has always been an intermediary for expressing our connection to the cosmos—matching the mystery of our own bodies to the mysteries of the universe helps us better understand both.

EAST MEETS WEST

This Indian temple plan show how many ancient Hindu sites translated the human body into architecture to create a symbolic representation of the cosmos.

BODY AS TEMPLE

This diagram is an extension of the temple plan on the left. The numbers on the body correlate to those on the different sections of the building plan. The correspondences are similar to Eastern Chakras, but instead of energy centers, the parts of the temple relate to parts of the body that sense or are similar to the function of the temple objects they refer to.

Many religions over the years have attempted to teach humanity the truth about the human body being a temple where the seat of the soul can be found surrounded by the wings of his inner angels like those of the Ark of the Covenant, the "Holy of Holies." There are illustrations which are found which outline the ancient notion that somehow humanity is perhaps one the most advanced machines to date housing within connection to the divine. When a person takes the time to look, they will find the answers hidden deep within. Edgar Cayce once said "Meditation is listening to the divine within."

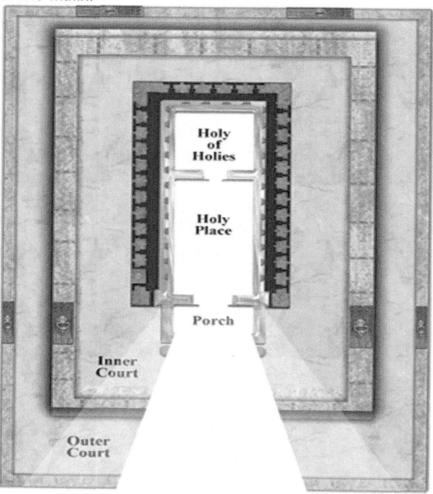

FINALE ANALYSIS

As our awareness of labyrinths and ourselves expands, it becomes more and more important to understand why these mysterious formations are popping up all over the world in the last couple of decades being placed on sacred landscapes, churches, schools, sacred monuments, and even in people's back yards. Perhaps there is becoming a growing awareness of the power contained therein and importance of labyrinths.

Besides having a mysterious background in history remarkably linked to the gods; the path tends to lead inward spiraling toward the center of self-realization. Once inside away from the mundane, the winding path tends to lead to a point of human spiritual transformation. The sacred practice of using labyrinths to get in touch with the adobe of the gods has been used for centuries by the ancients to connect humans on earth with those in the heavenly realms.

There have been a few people over the years who attempt to establish a working theory as to how the process actually works since the details are not only lengthy but some aspects are said to be closely guarded secrets. Nevertheless; the general hypothesis is when a person walks curtain labyrinths, they are essentially walking in the same path as its creator. The labyrinth creator once had a vision put forth into effort became an action resulting in an actuality of the creation of the labyrinth itself.

By walking the path in real life, first off, a reversal effect takes place. The walk recreates the labyrinth in the matrix of the mind on many levels of the person walking creating a spiritual blueprint in memory. With a one-pointed focus on the walk staying on the path the mind connects with the place forming visualizing of being in the mind of its creator on a subconscious and conscious level.

When taking a close look at labyrinths the general theme seems to be the same in most religions where everyone has their own definition of how these ancient devices are supposed to operate and overall purpose. Being that some are very old it's impossible to tell what the builders had in mind at the time leading to their construction. However, some labyrinths clearly stand out from all others like the *Chartres and Angel Valley Labyrinth*. Both contain the "Tree of Life" at its core. One is said to be the source having the Veil of Mary (Sancta Camisa) a piece of silk reported to have been worn during the Annunciation of Christ' birth by the angel Gabriel during her labor and delivery of Christos. The Chartres Labyrinth is the womb from which the Angel Valley Labyrinth was born. *Both oddly were according to legend blessed with the presence and assistance of Angels, Michael, and Gabriel.*

Normally people wouldn't even consider these kinds of claims of Angels assisting humans is the creation of such devices until one for themselves researches and digs a little deeper. The fact the Angel Valley Retreat Center at one time looked like some kind of galactic airport was an indication there may have been something to the claims. Now sightings have died down steadily declining after the 2012 arrival. Trying to explain why the area became so saturated is something people have been attempting to do for some time.

"Was it the Harmonic Convergence rumored to bring with it an assortment of spiritual gurus from around the world, Hollywood, or perhaps the Occultist who are known for summonsing entities and opening portals, or a combination?"

To some the Bradshaw Ranch across the street from Angel Valley is the twin to the Skinwalker Ranch in Utah. The underground caverns, strange sightings, and other supernatural events make one wonder as well.

One thing is for sure something was taking place in and around the Angel Valley Labyrinth shortly after it was built in the skies and on the ground enough to attract the *United States Government.* Congress does not normally buy up ranches, but for some mysterious reason they wanted the land directly around the Angel Valley Labyrinth.

Image above: The labyrinths path for some may seem like a huge leap of faith, however, to others the journey is real with uncommon roots leading deeper and deeper into the rabbit hole of who we are and beyond into our wildest imagination.

The Incarceration Labyrinth

The labyrinth symbolizes a journey to a predetermined destination (such as a pilgrimage to a holy site), or the journey through life from birth to a spiritual awakening to death. When it comes to those locked up in jail/prison a great opportunity exists in being able to help those who perhaps need it the most. People are supposed to be placed into jail/prison as punishment, not for further punishment, and therein lies a key and opportunity to being able to perhaps change people who have shown by actions they need some guidance. The pathway to change can often be difficult especially when some don't think they want or need the help, nevertheless, the labyrinth offers a clear path one step at a time for the message is found in the walking, "a sure path one step at a time."

When corrections officials are led down the path of the labyrinth after taking the walk themselves, many are amazed at what they find and experience. Experiencing the effects themselves corrections officials have began to see the benefits of having these mystical symbols inside their institutions.

Placing inmates on a good path *Sheriff Robert J. Garvey* the Superintendent of Hampshire County Jail and House of Corrections have become advocates of the benefits of labyrinth in correctional settings becoming "*sold from the first time and was convinced this thing had much more power than I would ever imagine.*"

Many have recognized throughout the years in the corrections industry doing time and wasting time need not go hand in hand. Meditation labyrinths are gaining popularity as a pathway to mental health and clarity showing up in hospitals and even jails/prisons. With 1 out of every 100 people in the United States behind bars, prison volunteers of all kinds are more important and more needed than ever. *A busy inmate is a happier inmate and a happier inmate is easier to manage.*

The Labyrinth makes itself available to inmates in the treatment program for those dealing with issues like substance abuse, anxiety, etc., which is a good relaxation tool for stress management in an environment of noise. The opportunity to get some quiet time in a safe place for many of the incarcerated is a golden moment. For people incarcerated the journey can be one of constant anxiety. As a counterpoint, labyrinths provide a refuge.

Inmates who come once to walk the walk of the labyrinth usually return again and again because it is the one place in their crowded, regimented routines where they can find quiet for personal reflection giving inmates the opportunity to stop and think, to reflect in a safe, quiet, and relatively stress-free zone.

As the pandemic has heightened stress and anxiety for many Americans, some feeling confined like those in prison, this form of moving meditation can be an escape. The magic of walking the path with its twists, to the left, then to the right, and an eventual turn into a center the labyrinth creates a calm within for many, easing whatever thoughts or concerns anyone may have one step at a time.

"Some small studies suggest that walking labyrinths can reduce distress in county jails/prisons for prisoners and hospitalized psychiatric patients as well as staff."

For those who may be incarcerated reading this now I am including a couple Chartres Labyrinths below for you and another (this is a good share) to trace with a pen or pencil. Once you understand the principles behind the symbol tracing it is the same as walking it for it is all done in *Mind, Body, and Spirit*.

Combining the imagery of the circle and the spiral into a purposeful path, labyrinths have long been used as meditation and prayer tools as a part of the pilgrimage path to wholeness and holiness. Labyrinths have been used for thousands of years–by the Romans and medieval monks, amongst others–as a religious practice, a way to find calm and ease within from the stresses without designed to calm and atone, for meditation and pilgrimage.

Your life is a sacred journey, you are the path. And from here, you can only go forward, not behind, able to shape your life story into a magnificent tale of discovery, change, growth continuously expanding your vision of what is possible, ultimately stretching your soul.

The nature of following the path, the small amount of concentration while walking, produces a calming effect, as reported by some "can do everything from reducing anxiety to combat chemotherapy-induced nausea." Which makes it perfect for a pandemic, people incarcerated, in hospitals, the disabled, and so on. Just about everyone can benefit from the labyrinth.

The Vortex Phenomena

Throughout the 80s a considerable amount of attention had developed towards understanding vortexes. What is said to happen when people visit these vortexes according to the new age community in Sedona is that one can be healed spiritually and even physically. Vortexes are areas of energy that are reported to rise up from the earth's surface, supposedly spiritually thus physically affecting any spiritually sensitive person who travels within the vicinity.

Systems of ley lines vortexes/portals is not a new idea. Sacred temples of the ancient world around the Mediterranean are located at powerful vortexes, and drawing lines between them will bring out patterns of triangles. The Indians in the American Southwest, as well as those in Peru and other parts of South America, located their cities and the roads between them on vortexes and ley lines.

Many sacred temples and churches have been built near or on powerful vortexes. Recently, NASA reported finding hidden portals in the Earth's magnetic field. It turns out there are 'hidden portals' in our planet's Magnetic field. According to scientists, it turns out that not only do portals actually exist but NASA-funded researchers at the University of Iowa to solve the mystery. "They're places where the magnetic field of Earth connects to the magnetic field of the Sun, creating an uninterrupted path leading from our own planet to the sun's atmosphere 93 million miles away." NASA has apparently stated the strange portals open and close several times a day. "Oddly, the UFO/Paranormal field have claimed for years the sun is part of a gigantic Star Gate used by *Gods* or highly advanced extraterrestrial civilizations to travel across the universe."

Many people report feeling the local vortex energy on some level within themselves, whether it is simply on a physical level, of increased energy and aliveness, increased mental clarity, or understanding of things that may come to them that were not there before. Some report obtaining new directions to take in life, solutions to problems, or new creative endeavors. The energies of vortexes some say can affect people on an emotional or spiritual level of feeling the presence of God/Source or having spiritual experiences. Many people report feeling the release of old emotions and sufferings that have been carried for a long time only to replace them with new awareness and understanding of things allowing them to begin anew.

The beauty of Sedona is such that many people can only compare it to a powerful spiritual experience. People from all over the world come to the area to experience the vortexes. You could say Sedona is the *"Vortex Capital"* of the world since so many people visit each year. To visit Sedona, you either have to recalibrate your sense of awe, or your brain interprets the experience as literally supernatural. If you're inclined to believe in the supernatural, then it's normal and expected for human psychology to determine that a higher power is in effect in Sedona.

The concept of the "energy vortex" is, for whatever reason, the popular explanation that took the strongest hold here. The magnitude of the experience is palpable enough that many of us tend to accept the vortex explanation as plausible. The feeling is strong thus the evidence seems to support the suggested explanation. However, few questions remain to be answered:

Is it possible —as legends suggest— these ancient sites were designed by intelligent forces going beyond rational understanding and that they are in fact ancient portals leading towards distant places elsewhere?

If there is an intelligent design behind vortexes, then who put them there and for what intended purpose?

Or are legends that speak of such portals nothing but ancient myths?

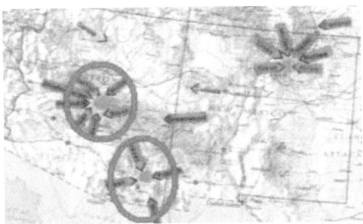

Image above: According to the Missing 411 research the Verde Valley and Mount Graham region are where people are vanishing and or perishing under suspicious circumstances. (Public domain)

Was it a coincidence David Paulides, a police officer for over 20 years and author of Missing 411, created a map after careful research bringing to light clusters of missing people throughout the United States discovering the Sedona/Verde Valley region was in his estimation the hot spot to go missing in the whole state?

Or how about the Sedona region having magnetic anomalies, whole mountain ranges, 500 times greater than the surrounding areas, was this normal?

After exploring the Sedona/Verde Valley region for over 20 years as a researcher and author running down some of the local myths and legends, specifically the vortex energy phenomena in relation to the extremely high magnetic anomalies found in the region, out of curiosity went one day to visit the Angel Valley Labyrinth. *"The experience was completely out of this world and phenomenal."*

Had visited all the other major vortex locations over the years ended up being disappointed having never felt a thing until I stepped into the Angel Valley Labyrinth after walking the walk. The *Sedona Chapel of the Holy Cross* is a good experience but nothing in comparison. All the legends/rumors/myths were real. Before visiting the Angel Valley Labyrinth totally did not buy into the vortex energy at all. It's the only place out of all in Arizona where something was experiential and boy was it.

Image above: Inside the *Matangeshvara Temple* sits what some consider to be another perfect example of the use of an enchanted labyrinth portal set in stone. (Public domain)

The Matangeshvara Labyrinth

Built sometime in 900-925 CE, with Ganesha statue at the entrance, the Matangeshvara temple is a Shiva temple in the Khajuraho town of Madhya Pradesh, India housing in stone what some consider to be an ancient device used as a portal to travel between dimensions. The only Hindu temple that is still actively used for worship in the region classified as a *Monument of National Importance by the ASI*.

According to the mythological accounts surrounding the creation of this mysterious structure, dedicated to Lord Shiva (the great Lord who has conquered death) housing the largest Shiva Linga in India, a sage named *Matanga* who manifested in form of a lingam, meaning of "evidence, proof" of God and God's existence.

The union of lingam and yoni represents the "indivisible two-in-oneness of male and female, the passive space and active time from which all life originates." The lingam and the yoni have been interpreted as the male and female sexual organs since the end of the 19th century by some scholars, while to practicing Hindus they stand for the inseparability of the male and female principles and the totality of creation. At a more subtle level, the Shiva lingam is the union of Prakriti (active energy) and Purusha (consciousness). According to the traditions Shakti allows consciousness to materialize, to become manifest. All things are created by this union and nothing can exist or change without it. It is the union of mind and soul. It also physically symbolizes the male and the female reproductive organs in a state of bliss.

There is a mysterious power (or Shakti) associated with the Linga same as the labyrinth. It is believed to induce concentration of the mind and help focus one's attention which is why the sages and seers of India prescribed Linga to be installed in the temples of Lord Shiva. In the post-Vedic period, the Linga became symbolical of the generative power of Lord Shiva into infinity.

Image above: Set in stone is Lord Shiva appearing within a pillar of light. This pillar is 9-foot tall anchored under the labyrinth structure as if to be ready to travel into the poral. (Public domain)

The Linga is not merely a block of stone for devotees, it is all-radiant able to communicate raising practitioners above body-consciousness assisting in communicating with the Lord therein. Scholars have been worshiping the golden Linga for its mystical powers for centuries. Coincidentally found set in stone is Lord Shiva within a pillar of light. This sign speaks volumes showing specifically in relation to the large 9-foot-high structure ironically sitting underneath the entrance to what appears to be some type of gateway. These mysterious structures display a host of symbolism as well as advanced workmanship. It's clear the creator wanted to convey a message.

Image above: Inside the magnetic structure of CERN where some are seeking the secrets of the universe, while to others such devices created to look into other dimensions maybe opening the portals of hell with its 666 logo a statue of Lord Shiva. (Public Domain)

Supernatural Gateways

Throughout history, there have been many legends of supernatural gateways existing where gods are mysteriously able to appear manifesting themselves like being transported on *Star Trek* materializing on a transporter pad. The remarkable aspect is when people begin to find structures centuries old which according to legend has the ability for traveling to otherworldly places.

CERN, a world-class fundamental physics research organization in Europe, operates a network of accelerators and a decelerator. The LHC consists of a 27-kilometer (17 miles) ring of superconducting magnets with a number of accelerating structures to boost the energy of the particles along the way through a loop at the speed of light looking for the "God particle."

Located in a place that was once called "Appolliacum" which some claim is Greek for destruction. In Roman times the place is said to be where they believed a gateway was to the underworld. Efforts to investigate extra dimensions and parallel universe through the LHC for many is ultimately where science meets religion.

CERN's ability to open and peer through doorways into other dimensions was made public on June 16, 2016, when the AWAKE (Advanced WAKEfield Experiment) project to accelerate charged particles took place then later a photographer posted a series of photos of the skies above showing a strange cloud formation and electrical activities. The media was soon in a frenzy about "portals" in the sky indicating CERN was responsible for opening parallel universes in extra dimensions.

Image above: Gudimallam Lingam dated to between the 3rd and 1st century BCE depicts Shiva with an antelope and axe in his hands standing over a demon in a beam of light. (Public domain)

Throughout history, there is plenty of evidence to show mankind has very been interested in discovering pathways to otherworldly places building elaborate structures to house these doorways. Without question, these places do in fact exist and are by no means to be taken lightly or played with. The ancient texts, artwork, statues, and other means have all spoken in detail of the dangers associated with what lies on the other side through the dimensional doorways.

We are warned in the *Holy Bible* and other ancient texts of the dangers which lie beyond God's protection. There are indeed forces which guard the gateways. Over and over, the texts state it takes a true guru or master in order to be able to safely travel into these otherworldly places because of the dangers therein in what lies beyond. What truly lies within the labyrinth is something each person is going to have to discover for themselves.

The End or is it the Beginning…

"SKYNET BECAME SELF-AWARE AND LEARNED TO TIME TRAVEL IN 2021 IRONICALLY AT THE SAME TIME THE BOOK BY MIKE DAVIS WAS RELEASED CALLED "THE ANGEL VALLEY LABYRINTH."

The Labyrinthian Path

At twilight, many enter the misty haze, inward towards a single star, they gaze.

Paying the required toll that they may play, drifting within hoping to find one's way.
Some say there's sanctity in solitude, and fortunes found within fortitude.
Walking mindfully the path by intent, wise to the journey of rhythm is sent.
With each step exploring the corridor, numberless winding passages to explore.
Twists and turns opening into one another, through the unknown, all advance as others.
Entering the serpentine path of thought, a mad person had these walls upbrought!
Within the echoing voids of the mind's eye, some are forever trapped while others do fly.
Looking within the labyrinth may seem deep, for answers like it's a game of hide-&-seek.
Seeking some perpetual truth about the game, why some are left to ponder Angel's fame.
Without a compass, there is the mind's wrath, of losing one's self in the labyrinthian path.
Narrow is the gateway ever-complex and deep, each night the dreamer enters whilst asleep.

End Notes: These are the notes from the first edition as updates will be added.

ABOUT THE AUTHOR

For over 20 years Mike Davis along with other likeminded individuals has been researching strange phenomena in the Sedona/Verde Valley region publishing those finding in publications and for the Verde Valley Vortex.

Made in the USA
Middletown, DE
11 January 2023

21330068R00096